PART 1

Support

Understand where you are now and where you want to be

CHAPTER 1

Starting to think about anger

Overview

This chapter is designed to get you thinking about anger:

- about how anger in general can be a positive force in your life if properly managed
- about your relationship with anger and your reasons for wanting to look at this relationship now
- about examples of people who came to the point where they needed to think about their relationship with anger
- about the challenge of doing this.

Introducing anger management

This book is not about doing away with anger. It is about helping you to change your relationship with anger. Anger has had a bad press. That is because people confuse anger with what it can lead to: violence, threats, fights etc. Anger is a *feeling*. Violence and threats are *behaviours*. Anger does not need to lead to those behaviours and that is what this book is about. On its own, anger is a vital resource. It protects us by alerting us to situations that are threatening (or at least, situations that feel threatening). It gets us ready to meet those threats. Unfortunately, it can take over. More precisely, we can allow it to take over, leading to behaviours such as violence and threats, and to unhealthy levels of stress. It does not need to be like that.

How to Deal with
Anger

Isabel Clarke

JOHN
MURRAY
LEARNING

First published in Great Britain in 2016 by John Murray Learning. An Hachette UK company.

Copyright © Isabel Clarke 2016

The right of Isabel Clarke to be identified as the Author of the Work has been asserted by her in accordance with the Copyright, Designs and Patents Act 1988.

Database right Hodder & Stoughton (makers)

British Library Cataloguing in Publication Data: a catalogue record for this title is available from the British Library.

Library of Congress Catalog Card Number: on file.

Paperback ISBN 978 1 47361671 4

eBook ISBN 978 1 47361673 8

1

The publisher has used its best endeavours to ensure that any website addresses referred to in this book are correct and active at the time of going to press. However, the publisher and the author have no responsibility for the websites and can make no guarantee that a site will remain live or that the content will remain relevant, decent or appropriate.

The publisher has made every effort to mark as such all words which it believes to be trademarks. The publisher should also like to make it clear that the presence of a word in the book, whether marked or unmarked, in no way affects its legal status as a trademark.

Every reasonable effort has been made by the publisher to trace the copyright holders of material in this book. Any errors or omissions should be notified in writing to the publisher, who will endeavour to rectify the situation for any reprints and future editions.

This book is for information or educational purposes only and is not intended to act as a substitute for medical advice or treatment. Any person with a condition requiring medical attention should consult a qualified medical practitioner or suitable therapist.

Typeset by Cenveo® Publisher Services.

Printed and bound in Great Britain by CPI Group (UK) Ltd., Croydon, CR0 4YY.

John Murray Learning policy is to use papers that are natural, renewable and recyclable products and made from wood grown in sustainable forests. The logging and manufacturing processes are expected to conform to the environmental regulations of the country of origin.

Carmelite House
50 Victoria Embankment
London EC4Y 0DZ
www.hodder.co.uk

CONTENTS

Acknowledgements — vi

Part 1: Support

Chapter 1: Starting to think about anger — 2

Chapter 2: The anger trap — 12

Chapter 3: Facing reality and commitment to change — 23

Part 2: Tackle

Chapter 4: Taking control of your body — 38

Chapter 5: Now you have a choice! — 52

Chapter 6: Using choice wisely — 67

Part 3: Escape

Chapter 7: Wind-up thinking — 86

Chapter 8: Alternatives to wind-up thinking — 100

Chapter 9: Letting go of chronic stress — 115

Chapter 10: Obstacles and consolidation — 135

Part 4: Practice

Chapter 11: Managing relationships differently — 152

Chapter 12: Relating differently to yourself — 167

Chapter 13: Your personal rules and values — 182

Part 5: Progress

Chapter 14: Using anger's energy to fulfil your potential — 200

Chapter 15: Keeping up progress — 215

Chapter 16: Useful resources and further help — 236

References — 241

Index — 245

Acknowledgements

I would like to acknowledge my debt to all those involved in the Anger Management Programme which ran between about 1993 and 2004 at the Department of Psychiatry in Southampton; that is, both the group participants and the many trainee facilitators. They were my main teachers in the subject of anger.

Preface

My qualification for writing this book is my experience of running an anger management programme for an inner-city psychological therapies service. I say more about this in Chapter 1. I am very aware that such services are often not available. Indeed, the one I set up folded when our service was no longer allowed to offer anything to people without a specific diagnosis. But anger is not a diagnosis. It is a human emotion (in common with diagnoses such as depression, anxiety, etc.) that can cause real problems and real distress, both to the individual with the identified 'anger' problem and to those around them. Anger also has the potential to be an important resource for good in the world if properly managed. For all these reasons, I can see the value in making available in book form a programme like the one my colleagues and I delivered. I do hope you find it useful.

The book is written with the assumption that the reader wants to work on a problem with anger. That may not be true for everyone who reads it. You might want to help or understand someone with such a problem. You might be more generally interested in understanding and helping people with an anger problem. But wherever you sit on that spectrum, I invite you to use the book also to think about your own relationship with anger.

When I was training staff to run anger management groups, I always got them to discuss their relationship with anger. Some said they didn't have one ('I am not an angry person') but by the end of the session, they had come to understand that everyone has a relationship to their anger – and not recognizing this isn't necessarily a good thing!

About this book

How to Deal with Anger features the **STEP P**ast method for overcoming anger. **STEP P**ast is a five-step approach, drawing on cognitive behavioural therapy techniques, that gives practical and emotional support to anyone affected by anger issues.

S – Support helps you come to terms with the problem, and maps out the road to recovery.

T – Tackle the negative thoughts and behaviour patterns that hold you back.

E – Escape the behaviours and situations that make your life a struggle.

P – Practice provides coping strategies to help you adjust your responses and replace harmful thoughts, when they occur.

P – Progress to a healthier, happier new life – without fear of setbacks or relapse.

Worksheets from this book are available free online at www.teachyourself.com/howtodealwith when you purchase the book.

Case studies

None of the case studies quoted here represents one single individual. By the time I came to write this book, I was too far removed from the service to find the people concerned and gain consent for that. Instead, I have used examples of situations, reactions etc. from many people and put them together in examples that illustrate both the points to be made and the many ways in which people react to their anger that I witnessed during my time running the programme.

Anger and electricity

Think of anger as like electricity. Two hundred years ago, before the discovery and harnessing of electricity, what did people know about electricity? They knew about lightning strikes – disastrous! And they were perhaps familiar with static electricity – a bit of a nuisance. When this knowledge was put together to harness electrical currents, it became the mainstay of our comfort and survival that it is today.

Like electricity, anger represents energy – it mobilizes our body for action to meet a threat. Anger management is about using that energy – to take our lives forward; to realize our potential – by not allowing it to be frittered away in harmful violence or bitter brooding over wrongs.

Anger: good and bad things list

Worksheet 1A

How does the idea that there are good as well as bad things about anger strike you? Make two lists: one of good things about anger, the other of bad things about anger.

Good things about anger	Bad things about anger

So, if managing anger is so much of a no-brainer, why is the world full of angry people and violence? There are good reasons for this. It is fundamental to being human. Imagine a world where human beings always behave rationally and emotions and relationships are always straightforward. Is it recognizable? What would the stories, films, soap operas etc. of that world be like? No, as human beings, we inevitably struggle to manage the most important aspects of our lives because of the way our brains are wired and connected to our bodies. When we feel up against it, it is easy for us to get a wrong or unhelpful idea, and for our body to take over and act on that unhelpful idea. This will be examined further in Chapter 2.

In the case of anger, this combination of brain and body can get us locked in a vicious circle where the anger takes over and dictates what we do and how we see the world – leading to more anger. Over time, this comes to feel normal. Learning a different relationship with your anger, which is the subject of this book, means learning a new way of managing the world. This is challenging. It takes courage and commitment. It is worth it!

Anger management group programmes

I am confident that learning to manage anger is worthwhile because of my experience of over 10 years of running an anger management programme as part of an inner city psychological therapy service. We put on regular group programmes. I assessed most of the people for the groups and supervised the staff running them – doctors, psychologists and nurses who were learning about cognitive behavioural therapy (CBT). We published a thorough evaluation of the groups, demonstrating that they did help people achieve a better relationship with their anger, and another paper about how we organized the service (Bradbury and Clarke, 2006; Naeem et al., 2009). What convinced me even more than the questionnaires that we used to establish that it was useful, was the change I saw in the lives of those who stuck with the programme and took the message home. For example, one group member who phoned us a year after he finished the programme; his car had been stolen, with all the handouts and papers from the programme in it – he was desperate to get a replacement set as he used them constantly to keep his life on track.

Not everyone did complete the course; every group had its drop-outs. However, these people generally did not leave because they thought the programme was useless, but at the point when they could see it would work – they saw other people making changes in their lives and did not feel ready for that challenge themselves.

Most people come to anger management because of the damage that their anger is doing to their lives and their relationships. They might notice how much their anger is hurting those they love. More often, they cannot immediately see that, but they recognize that they stand to lose really important things: partners, children, jobs, liberty.

When I assessed people for inclusion in the group programme, we discussed what had brought them to seek help with anger. Sometimes it became clear that seeking help with their anger was not really their agenda but was important to those around them. Where this turned out be the case, we concluded that now would not be the best time to enter the programme – there would be time for that when they were ready in the future; when they really wanted to change, and were not just giving in to pressure.

Others could see how much their anger was damaging their lives, how much they stood to lose if they did not tackle it, but were understandably concerned about having to change how they managed their lives. They usually joined the programme. Some stuck it. Others didn't. A third group were really sure that this was the chance they needed. Along with some of the second group, they generally did well.

Case study: Pam (1)

Pam was the nerve centre of a busy independent taxi firm. Her employer valued her ability to keep the drivers up to the mark and the fares rolling in. He also valued the way the cheerfully efficient Pam kept an unruly bunch of drivers on their toes with her notoriously vile temper. As the middle one of three sisters of a single mother, she had needed this temper when growing up to create space for herself and get heard between her elder sister, who was her mother's companion, and the indulged baby sister. However, when she and Barry, her partner of 10 years, decided to start a family in their mid thirties, life was turned upside down for Pam. Stuck at home with a new baby and missing the bustle of the job, when the screaming did not stop even after the little so-and-so had been fed, changed, given every comfort … Pam forced herself to leave him in the cot and go out as she was convinced that if she picked him up she would shake … and hard. That evening, she told Barry she needed to do something about her anger. It was vital that she could control her temper for the sake of her son. However, if she stopped being fiery Pam, would she still be the same person? What would that do to her performance in her job?

What has led you to pick up this book? Is it for yourself? Or do you want to support someone else to change their relationship with their anger?

Self-assessment ✓

Worksheet 1B

What has made tackling anger important to you at this point in time? List whatever reasons come to mind, and then rate each item on your list. Give the biggest factor a 1 and so on.

Then list any concerns you might have about tackling your anger. You could rate those too.

Reasons to tackle your relationship with anger	Rating	Concerns about tackling it	Rating

To get the most out of this book, it is no good just skimming through it. You need to use the worksheets. Have a pen handy. Write things down. Or if you are not a writing person, get a recording device and record your answers. Don't skip bits if you want this book to work for you.

Anger and relationships

All our emotions – love, fear, guilt, jealousy and, of course, anger – are about managing relationships. The most obvious example of that is where you are angry with other people. You feel that they might be a threat to things that are important for you; that they are not treating you fairly or, more generally, not doing what they 'should' do. It could also be that you feel threatened by an institution (government bodies frequently feature here) or even an idea.

The central relationship that people often fail to notice is their relationship with themselves, because all human beings are a relationship. Think about it. Notice how we think naturally in a conversation with ourselves. That relationship can vary as much as the relationships with the people around us. Often people are very hard on themselves. Some people really do not like themselves very much. Angry people are frequently angry with themselves as well as with others.

This side of anger often remains hidden. Some people are not even really aware of it – it is just a drag on their lives – leading to stress and depression. When people turn their anger against themselves, it can lead to behaving self-destructively; examples of this are giving in to drink or drugs. Or it can mean that they do not allow themselves to make use of their potential; treating themselves badly and not giving themselves a chance just seems right in the light of how they feel about themselves.

If anything is really going to change, tackling the relationship between you and you is key. If you can set aside all those negative opinions about yourself and commit to treating yourself right, a whole lot of things will fall into place. As with all real change, this is easier to say than to do. Your relationship with yourself will be a well-worn habit, and can probably be traced back to the way other people treated you in the past – often the distant past.

This is where a little anger, carefully applied to the problem, can supply the courage you need to change. Why should you remain stuck in the past? It probably was not that good. You need to give yourself a chance to cope differently in the present, and you are not going to manage that if you continue to pull yourself down, in the same way that others did way back.

Self-assessment ✓

Worksheet 1C

What is your relationship with yourself like? If you think it could do with some work, write down some of things you find yourself saying to yourself.

_____

_____

_____

_____

_____

_____

Are the things you say to yourself critical and discouraging? Ask yourself, would you say those things to a good friend?
What would you say to a good friend who was struggling? Write that down.

_____

_____

_____

_____

_____

_____

Try saying it to yourself. What does that feel like?

If you object that you do not deserve it etc., recognize that you might not be the person you would like to be or might not have achieved what you wanted precisely because you have always put yourself down and not given yourself a chance.

Running away from yourself

Another thing that people do who have a bad relationship with themselves is to try to escape. Being them feels really uncomfortable. Our society offers lots of ways of escaping the uncomfortable feeling. Alcohol is perhaps the most available. Street drugs, gambling and pornography are other examples of the many tempting options. The fact that all these are harmful if used to excess can add to their attraction in escaping from how it feels to be you – for someone who dislikes themselves, harming themselves can feel right and natural, even a relief.

All these things work in the short term to help someone cope with horrible feelings. In the longer term, they keep the person locked into a bad relationship with themselves and, even worse, make it very hard to change anything. Because these ways of coping are so 'successful', they are very addictive – given half a chance they will take over someone's life. Also, in order to change well-established habits, it is essential to have a clear head. To make changes, you need to be able to notice what you are doing, then notice what you are about to do, and then choose to do something different. You cannot do that if you are out of it in any way.

Case study: Josh (1)

Josh had always felt picked on and resentful. A black kid from an inner-city estate, he had managed being bullied at school by becoming a bully. He was bright and his teachers wanted him to develop his aptitude for maths and science and go to university, but the rewards of money and acceptance to be gained through dealing drugs used his talents in a more immediate way. He felt regular cannabis use was essential to calm a temper that threatened his relationship, which was deeply important for him. Carmen really believed in him and wanted him to make something of himself outside the criminal world, for herself and their daughter. Though the cannabis made him chill in the evenings, the temper woke up again next day, along with self-hatred as a part of him knew that this was not the right life. Cocaine distracted and supplied excitement, but led to irrational jealousy. After a violent episode, witnessed by their daughter, frightened both Carmen and Josh, and deepened Josh's underlying self-loathing, he sought help for his anger.

The therapist expressed doubt that Josh could successfully use the cognitive behavioural approach, which requires a clear head all the time, if he continued with a heavy cannabis habit. He had to recognize that she had a point. Although cannabis made Josh mellow in the evening, it was probably linked to his jumpiness next day. He recognized the problem with cocaine, but in his social group and with the lifestyle he had, giving up drugs looked well nigh impossible.

Josh was faced with a choice. His relationship with a woman he loved and who believed in his potential, not just his current earning power, and with his little girl, whom he adored, were in one corner; his whole way of life, including how he managed the world and his conflicted feelings about himself, was in the other. Getting from here to there was not going to be easy. Was Josh ready to change his lifestyle and face his demons?

Obstacles to change list

Worksheet 1D

What would it be like for you to make real changes in your relationship with anger?

_____

_____

_____

Is there anything getting in the way?

_____

_____

_____

What changes would you have to make first (e.g. reducing dependence on alcohol)?

_____

_____

_____

Is there anything that change would mean facing up to?

_____

_____

_____

Is there anything you would need to let go of (e.g. a lifestyle that would get in the way of making changes)?

_____

_____

_____

Chapter summary

After reading Chapter 1, you should be able to:

- see anger as something with the potential to be useful to you, but which can take over if you do not take charge
- have some idea of how this happens, which is to do with the fundamentals of being a human being
- have thought about your relationship with anger
- have thought about your relationship with yourself
- have thought about the costs and benefits of tackling your relationship with anger – of starting to take back control of yourself and your life.

The other chapters in this book go more deeply into the way that anger operates and manages to take control so firmly. They offer plenty of opportunity, along with practical skills and strategies, to help you take back control so that you, and not your anger, are in charge!

CHAPTER 2

The anger trap

Overview

This chapter is about understanding more about anger and the way it can get a grip on your life. It looks at:

- the connection between a sense of threat and the body – how it is that the body and the feelings can take over
- how past threat gets mixed up with the present
- anger as a way of coping with life – a way of coping that probably worked well once
- the addictive side of anger
- starting to track in more detail where anger fits into your life, as a first step towards taking back control for yourself.

Certainty and threat

There are some things that all human beings would like. They would like control over and certainty about the important aspects of their life: somewhere to live, an adequate income, a loving family. Unfortunately, life is rarely that certain. As pointed out in Chapter 1, it would be a strange world if all the important aspects of our lives could be managed with certainty. Feeling under threat is a common human experience. The tiny baby feels under threat of certain death when the next feed is a little late, and it lets everyone know exactly how it is feeling with frantic crying. As we grow older, we have more sense of how the world works, but often enough that does not feel comfortable. Children of school age can be quite cruel; parents can sometimes come to the end of their tether and punishment gets out of hand. Sometimes this means that physical threat is a reality – children get hit. Emotional threat – the sense that important people are cross and so do not love you any more – is another common experience. Then there is threat to how you fit in with other people. How do you measure up compared with them? Remember your first day at a new school? Anxieties about whether you would be liked and accepted, or whether you could get away without being beaten up?

That sense of threat is important for human beings. They have not come this far in terms of evolutionary success without becoming really good at responding to threat. Our bodies are geared up to react rapidly to threat. The problem now, though, is that our bodies are still stuck in the Stone Age when it comes to the sort of threat they are geared up to react to. Fight or flight, attacking or running away, is ideal when faced with a sabre-toothed tiger. But faced with a traffic jam, a demanding boss or a disagreement with your partner, it is less useful. Our sophisticated, modern world is not like the environment our early ancestors lived in. We have built this world with our intelligence and used our abilities to tame that brutal Stone Age environment. Why can't we manage ourselves as efficiently as we can manage the world around us? Why can that primitive threat reaction still take over so easily?

It is because the part of our brains that manages the threat system is separate from the sophisticated thinking part – and when in doubt, it is the threat system that takes over! The States of mind 1 box explains this.

States of mind 1: there is no boss

Being human is difficult – this was stated in Chapter 1. We are now going to look at why. It is all to do with the way our brains are wired. Everyone knows how panic and anger can take over and overwhelm clear, logical thinking. We have already looked at the way in which the body takes charge at these times, launching us into action. Too often it is action that calm reflection would judge to be a bad idea, but once the body has taken over, calm reflection goes out of the window.

This happens because our brain has different compartments that manage different aspects of our minds. Seeing, hearing, feeling – our senses – are one compartment. Verbally-based thinking is a separate one. There is a neat model of how all this hangs together: interacting cognitive subsystems (ICS) (Teasdale and Barnard, 1993). This model is based on over a decade of detailed research into memory and information processing. According to ICS, all these different compartments are managed by two main organizing systems. One connects with our sight, hearing, body – everything physical and emotional. The other one, which developed later in our evolutionary journey, manages our verbal, logical side. The verbal, logical brain circuitry can know things for sure. It is this, newer part of the brain that gives us our sense of being an individual.

The way in which the brain is organized gives us two distinct states of mind: the emotional one and the verbally based reasonable one. The crucial thing about the ICS model is that neither part of the mind is in overall control; there is no boss. Control is constantly handed back and forth between the different compartments. In some circumstances, when things are very stressful for example, they lose touch with each other. No wonder being human can be difficult!

Figure 2.1 is borrowed from dialectical behaviour therapy (DBT), a therapy devised by Marsha Linehan in the USA, which uses the idea of a balance, or dialectic, at its heart (Linehan, 1993). The diagram shows how the two parts of the mind are distinct but also overlap. Linehan calls the place where they overlap the 'Wise Mind'. This is not an easy place to find; you have to work at it. DBT makes extensive use of mindfulness to help you get there, and mindfulness is introduced in Chapter 5 of this book. I have added to Figure 2.1 a separate memory for each circle – more about that below.

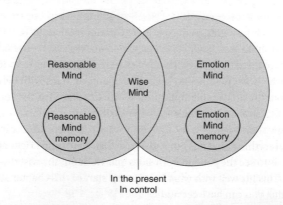

Figure 2.1: Different circuits in the brain (borrowed from DBT)

Because there is no overall 'boss' of our minds, we need to develop one if we are to be truly in control of our lives and able to steer our lives in the best way possible. But because we are pulled in different directions by our reason and our emotions, that 'boss' needs to be a negotiator rather than a dictator: to be able to listen to both sides and come to the best decision. That is what anger management is about. The threat system is important, but needs to be kept in check. Starting to notice what the threat system is up to is a central part of that.

Dialectical behaviour therapy

The states of mind diagram (Figure 2.1) and the concepts of the Reasonable Mind, Emotion Mind and Wise Mind run throughout this book, because they are such useful ideas and explain so much. For this reason, I am going to explain more about dialectical behaviour therapy (DBT) at this point. It is an approach that I have applied widely, and it is very relevant to anger management and many of the topics covered in this book. However, anger is not the problem that DBT was designed to address.

Marsha Linehan developed DBT specifically to help women with problems of self-harm and attempting suicide. It was first evaluated and shown to be effective for people with these problems, but has since been developed and applied much more widely. Linehan had her own experience of self-harm, and had not found the conventional therapies she was offered helpful. She drew on her interest in Buddhism to devise her own approach, which was rather different. Instead of getting people to talk about their feelings, as in a psychodynamic therapy, or to note and challenge their thoughts, as in cognitive behavioural therapy (CBT), she came up with skills classes to teach people to understand their emotions and manage them differently. The classes were backed up with individual therapy which was designed to keep participants on track with behaviour change. Buddhism gave her mindfulness (see Chapter 5) as the core skill to use, and also the idea of balance – the 'dialectic' that makes the name of the therapy sound rather scary. This is the idea that there are always two sides to everything, and it is rarely the case that there is one right answer. The trick is to see the good in both sides and work out the wisest way forward. This fits well with what I said at the start of this chapter about the illusion that you can have certainty.

The threat system and the body

The way in which the threat system takes over your body is covered in detail in Chapter 4. For now, you need to start to notice the changes that take place when you begin to feel angry. Also, your anger affects other people, and what they notice is also important. The next worksheet is for you to note what differences you feel and what changes other people also notice. They might sometimes tell you about it, for example:

Other: 'Why are you angry?'

Angry person: 'I'm not angry.'

Other: 'You're drumming your fingers, and tapping your foot'

or

Other: 'You're staring again – what are you angry about?'

If your significant other(s) have not told you (maybe they haven't dared ...), why not ask them?

Reviewing behaviour

Worksheet 2A

What changes do you notice in your body when you start to get angry?	What would others notice? (What do they report?)

Mixing up the past with the present

There is another reason why the threat system can get so out of hand. Not only does it come up with an over-simple solution (fight or run away) to complicated situations, but often it is reacting to threats that are not even in the present. They were real enough once, but they happened in the past. This is one of the peculiarities in the way our memory works, and another result of our brain wiring. See the States of mind 2 box!

States of mind 2: memory and time

The first States of mind box talked about the different compartments in the brain and identified the two states of mind: the emotional one and the verbally based reasonable one. But there is another complication. Each of these compartments has its own memory. This is shown in my version of the DBT states of mind diagram (Figure 2.1). Think of the quality of memory when you are, say, remembering a powerful physical experience – being in love; holding a new baby for the first time – or a frightening or anger-provoking experience. Enter into the memory. Can you feel your body getting involved?

Contrast this with the sort of memory you need in the exam room – for example, the written part of the driving test. The first sort of memory should bring things to mind really vividly. It might bring the body to life with some of the feelings we felt at the time. In the exam room, we are recalling facts, as drily and calmly as we can. That feels quite different.

So, we have two different types of memory: one is emotional and sensory; the other is verbal. Most importantly, only the verbal memory understands time. The two states of mind need to have connected for us to know when the sensory memory (love, baby, fear etc.) happened. Where, say, the fear was overwhelming, this connection might never have been made. So we may experience extreme memories from the past, often of situations when we were under real threat, as if they are happening now. This is called 'trauma memory' (Brewin et al., 1996). It explains why people who have been through very threatening experiences in the past, e.g. physical abuse in childhood, can have problems with fear and anger in the present. It all comes flooding back when there is a sense of threat in the present. The danger is that their reaction belongs more to the past than to the present.

It follows from this that when the threat system kicks in and your body starts to get ready to meet that threat, it might not be reacting wholly to what is going on now. Something that is happening now will have started it off – someone has said something, the situation looks threatening in some way – but this might have triggered your reaction to a really threatening situation you found yourself in way back in the past, even in childhood. Your reaction will make sense to you in that moment, but to everyone else it will not. It will look like a serious overreaction.

Think about your anger.

- Does it always fit with what is happening now?
- Could the past be getting in the way (as it did in the case of Lisa that follows).

Recall recent times when you have felt angry. Did any memories of similar things happening in the past come to mind? Could they have influenced how you felt in the present? Made it worse?

Case study: Lisa

Lisa was a talented dancer, and very much in love with Rob, who adored her. But there was a problem. She found it impossible to trust Rob. She worked herself up into a fury thinking that he was being unfaithful. Only after she had calmed down could she see how unfair she was being to him. Sometimes she would wake in the night and, half asleep, attack him vigorously.

This was Lisa's past getting in the way of her present life. As a teenager, she had escaped a violent and unloving home through marriage to an older man who promised her everything, but turned out to be sadistic, controlling and unfaithful. After several years of hell, Lisa managed to escape, pursue her dream career, and meet Rob. It was often when things seemed at their most perfect that something would trigger the vivid memories of the fear and hatred that marked her former relationship. She would be gripped by the conviction that Rob was cheating, or would half wake from sleep to fight him as she had fought for her life when assaulted by her former husband.

Desperate to make the relationship work, Lisa sought anger management. The therapist assessing her referred her first for individual therapy to enable her to meet and come to terms with the terrifying things she had lived through that kept breaking into her current life.

How anger gets a grip on your life

Anger can get a real grip on a person's life:

- even when someone can recognize that their anger is often out of proportion
- even when it might have more to do with the past than the present
- even when it is getting in the way of important relationships.

It can be really hard to break free of it.

One reason for this goes back to the issue of control mentioned at the start of this chapter. Anger can appear to come to the rescue in a world that is threatening and hard to control. It is when anger initially seems to work well that it is particularly dangerous. Compare it with how the gambler gets hooked. Their first time at the casino or on the machines, the gambler has a really big win or a run of good luck. Of course they expect and want that again. That luck is bound not to last – after all, it is always the gambling establishment owner who wins in the end! But it is extremely hard to break free of what has become an addiction to the buzz of the uncertainty: whether this time will be the jackpot or not. Anger has the added ingredient of buzz from the adrenaline that rushes round the body when the threat system is activated. That in itself can be addictive. Another aspect is that letting go of that watchful, ready to meet the challenge, high-stress state can feel unsafe. Either way or both ways, someone can find themselves locked into using anger to manage their life, even if that is not what they really want. They are caught in the anger trap.

Case study: Mick (1)

Mick had a secret. The only people who knew it were his parents and his wife. His wife shielded him loyally and helped him to manage his life successfully without letting on that he was illiterate. Of course, when he was at school, it had been a horrible struggle – everyone else had access to a world that was closed to him. All the time he was expected to do things that he just couldn't begin to get to grips with. Worse, the other kids watched his struggles – because he really did want to keep up, to succeed, to please his parents – made fun of him mercilessly. He was the odd one out; the stupid one – a large, gentle boy, always trying to finish his work, nothing left for fun and games. They goaded him and attacked him, until he could take no more. He turned on five of them in a fury and hit out, badly hurting at least three. The others fled in fear. His reputation changed overnight. Suddenly no one messed with him. His protection was valued, and if a new boy or a new situation looked as if it might challenge his dominant status, he found that showing his threatening side soon put him back on top. As an adult, Mick was a pleasant and mild man most of the time, until, he claimed, he would suddenly switch and go ballistic – with no warning.

Mick's example shows how anger can switch from being a solution to becoming a trap.

Self-assessment ✓

Worksheet 2B: Caught in the anger trap?

Note down any of the points in the previous section that might apply to you.

Does the past get in the way of the present?

_____

_____

_____

_____

Is anger a solution that has become a habit?

_____

_____

_____

_____

Does anger sometimes feel good? Safe?

_____

_____

_____

_____

Giving up a way of coping that has worked in the past is not easy, so congratulate yourself if you are determined to give it a go. The first thing to tackle is starting to understand the role of anger in your present life by monitoring it as you go. To start on this, fill out Worksheet 2B. If you were attending a group, there would be a week between each session in which to complete the chart. There will be more about charts and monitoring in Chapter 3. For now, do give it a go.

By the way, 'I had a good week. I didn't get angry' won't work. If you kept your temper and did not go over the top – excellent. However, I am sure you felt somewhat miffed at times; things got under your skin a bit; you felt uneasy about something. It is important that you note and write down those little disturbances as well as the major bust-ups that, hopefully, will never happen (again?).

Reviewing behaviour

Worksheet 2C

Try to fill in one line each day. It is important that you notice and write down smaller disturbances – feeling slightly miffed, things getting under your skin, feeling uneasy about something – as well as any major experiences of anger.

Date and time	What was happening/ what happened	What did you notice in your body?	How did you react?

Chapter summary

After reading this chapter, you should:

- have some idea about the threat system and why and how it can take over
- understand the role of past threatening experiences in your current reactions
- understand the way in which anger can take over and become addictive
- have thought about how this might apply to you
- have started to monitor closely your own relationship with anger, as a first step towards taking back control from the threat system.

Facing reality and commitment to change

Overview

In this chapter you will be introduced to:

- using and building up the habit of monitoring your anger
- understanding what affects whether or not you lose your temper
- more about the brain and its part in what happens
- getting a deeper understanding of your relationship with anger as a preparation for working on change.

Monitoring your progress

I am so used to seeing anger management in terms of weekly groups that I find it hard to adjust to the idea that you might not have had a week between reading Chapter 2 and Chapter 3; you could be reading the whole book at one sitting – or have given up on it at first and then picked it up months later after that big row …

If you are using this book as an anger management course for yourself, I suggest that it will work best for you if you do read roughly a chapter a week and fill in the worksheets over the days between. However, I am aware that people do not always do what is suggested! If you happen not to have filled in Worksheet 2C at the end of Chapter 2, before launching into this chapter, please turn back to it, cast your mind back over the week and try to fill in some of the times when things affected you – even if there were no major bust-ups to report. Even if you don't want to write anything down, just think back over the week and remember what you would have written … I do realize that angry people are not always the most compliant!

Looking at the completed worksheet, what do you notice? Look first at the date and time column – very interesting that one. Do you see any patterns? For instance, you might notice that the incident always occurs when you have just returned home from work; perhaps things were not feeling quite right after a hard day? Or around your small children's bath time at about 6 p.m.? Or later in the evening after a few drinks? Noting any pattern in *when* your anger is activated will tell you when to watch out for your danger time.

Now look at the second column, about the situation. Are there any patterns there: particular people or particular situations that tend to spark that anger?

Looking at the third column about what you noticed in your body, pay attention to that and try to remember. That will be key to your success with anger management.

Look at the fourth column. How did you react? Maybe you can now be surprised at your restraint. Perhaps you can see that the threat system does not always take over. Your threat system might have been activated, but you managed to keep control of it. Maybe at other times that threat system would have taken over almost before you had time to notice. This chapter will look at what might be going on in such cases.

Anger management is all about you understanding yourself better so that you can take charge – by and by. We haven't got to those chapters yet … I know, angry people are usually impatient people.

Inhibition and disinhibition: when do you let your anger out?

A lot of people coming to anger management insist that they have no control over their anger: it comes on from nowhere and takes over. They take the line that it is up to other people to be aware of this and take responsibility for not pushing their buttons. However, when you probe deeper it becomes clear that there are some situations in which they regularly explode and others, where the annoyance is as great or greater, when they do not. Everyone can recognize the 'kick the cat' scenario – an individual comes home from a stressful day at work where he/she held it together and takes out the frustration on the poor pet (or, far too often, partner and children).

When interviewing people about their relationship to anger, it was important to explore this aspect. However much the individual felt their anger was out of control, some order, some rules, always emerged. Often they sought help when their anger had got out of hand and they had broken one of those rules. Interestingly, the rules were different for different people. One man would firmly declare: 'I would never hit a woman', but kept losing jobs because of getting into fights at work. Another would put up with untold irritations at work, but take it out on the folks at home. Some people tended to vent their frustration on weaker parties, others would face up to the stronger.

All these rules operated below the level of careful, conscious thinking – after all, they kicked in at times of loss of temper, which connects them with the basic brain function of inhibition and disinhibition: letting something happen and not letting it happen. This operates all the time at the level of neurones. First, it's time to apply this idea of rules, of inhibition and disinhibition, to yourself.

Inhibitions and disinhibitions list

Worksheet 3A

When it comes to inhibition, disinhibition and you, what are your rules? In what sorts of situations do you lose your temper (think of the last few occasions). Jot down some examples.

_____

_____

_____

_____

In what situations would you never, or very rarely, lose your temper? Jot down examples.

_____

_____

_____

_____

Where you feel angry in those situations, what happens to your anger? Think of recent examples.

_____

_____

_____

_____

What happened afterwards? See if you can discover some connections.

_____

_____

_____

_____

You might learn some interesting things about yourself!

Anger and the brain

Much has been written about the brain and the different functions of the different parts. However, the brain is very hard to study because it is so delicate and complicated. Until recently, most of the information came from noting the effects of damage to particular parts of the brain. New scanning techniques, such as positron emission tomography (PET) and magnetic resonance imaging (MRI) have greatly extended the scope for studying the brain; we now have access to pretty pictures of which parts light up when someone is thinking about particular things (provided they have drunk the requisite radioactive isotope). Even this, though, is still quite clumsy and only gives us brief snapshots. We do know that the emotions are organized from areas deep within the brain, such as the amygdala, and that our more deliberate thinking comes from the frontal cortex, the new brain. The evolutionary aspect of this has already been referred to.

However, to understand how the all-important inhibition and disinhibition factors work in anger, the way that the neurones pass information around to the different bits of the brain is significant. I hope the description in the box below helps to explain this.

The brain as a bureaucracy

Imagine the brain as two buildings next to each other, housing one huge bureaucracy, of the sort you need to run a large company or government department. It is full of endless corridors (neurones) and doors (synapses). Staff (neuronal impulses) glide along the corridors endlessly, and where they come across an open door they go in. Other doors are shut, or bang shut as they approach, so are avoided. Sometimes the corridors are really fast and the staff can skate along (a rush of adrenaline does that). Sometimes they are much slower and stickier. Wider connections are possible at those slower times because the staff stay on tried and tested routes at the times when the going is fast. Which doors are open and which are shut is determined by a host of factors. What the individual whose brain it is 'wants' is only one among the many factors, although important principles like 'Never hit a woman' slam the odd door. Alcohol and street drugs have a tendency to fling open all the doors; and prescribed psychotropic drugs act by affecting the doors, opening and shutting them in complex ways, but not always precisely or predictably.

There are two buildings because of the two major departments, Reasonable Mind and Emotion Mind, as described in Chapter 2. In my image, staff run constantly back and forth between the two buildings all day. They flow best between the buildings at the 'slower' times. At 'fast' times they tend not to bother with the Reasonable building, and there is just one door to each which can be closed. During sleeping times they do not connect and the doors are closed. The Reasonable building goes quiet, and while the Emotion one has the odd staff member tidying up and wandering around rather randomly. In fact, the whole thing is a bit random – remember, this is a bureaucracy with no boss!

Common disinhibitors

When you did the exercise about the times when you are more likely to lose your temper (Worksheet 2C), did you notice any patterns about when that was likely to happen? There are a number of common ones. Look and them and see which applies to you.

- Your body – a number of factors that affect how your body functions affect your irritability levels and your ability to manage anger, for example:
  - ▸ lack of sleep
  - ▸ hunger
  - ▸ pain
  - ▸ other ill-health
- The environment, for example:
  - ▸ uncomfortable heat or cold
  - ▸ noise
  - ▸ being put under pressure, by yourself or by others; too much happening or needing attention at once
- Substances, such as:
  - ▸ alcohol
  - ▸ street drugs
  - ▸ some prescribed medication, e.g. SSRI anti-depressants, can in certain circumstances and for certain people disinhibit anger.

Alcohol, drugs and aggression

When you look at scientific studies about an area that 'everybody' thinks they understand, obvious conclusions are often questioned and things turn out to be not as simple you might have thought. In the case of alcohol, there is general agreement that it has a disinhibiting effect – it loosens the brakes that stop people doing things. Alcohol is often associated with violent behaviour in people who, when sober, would not act like that. It is frequently implicated in incidents of domestic violence, aggressive disturbance in pubs, accident and emergency departments in hospitals and the like. Scientific studies suggest that this is not due simply to disinhibition of behaviour, but that the effect of disconnecting reasonable-mind thinking, and so losing the bigger picture and awareness of consequences, is possibly more important (Gillet et al., 2001). Cocaine, on the other hand, can have a direct disinhibition effect deep in the brain (the limbic system). Cannabis is more complex. Its main effect is calming but, particularly in heavy and regular use of strong strains, it can have other effects in some (but not all) users; for instance, where it produces paranoia (unreasonable fear of persecution), this can easily lead to aggression. The withdrawal effects from cannabis can also involve anxiety, agitation and so, sometimes, aggression.

None of these substances is likely to produce aggression from nowhere in a previously pacific individual, but where there is already a tendency to violence, the substances can take away some of the restraints. The moral is: if you want to be in control of your life and your behaviour, use alcohol only in strict moderation and cut out the rest!

Your disinhibitors list

Worksheet 3B

Look at the list of common disinhibitors again. Tick those that affect your temper and anger control.

Your body:

Lack of sleep	☐
Hunger	☐
Pain	☐
Other ill-health	☐

The environment:

Uncomfortable heat/cold	☐
Noise	☐
Being put under pressure, by yourself or by others	☐
Too much happening or needing attention at once	☐

Substance use:

Alcohol	☐

Case study: Mabel

Mabel was embittered about the lot fate had dealt her. In her early twenties she had been happy, married to a wonderful husband, with two small children – a lovely family, as everyone said. Then her husband was killed in an industrial accident. She was devastated. As well as having to bring up two toddlers alone, there was a battle for compensation, complicated by the collapse of the firm he had worked for, which left a legal morass and little money for the victims. At first she was fighting along with other relatives caught up in the accident, but that group fell away after the (inadequate) pay-out, and in any case, she was the only one to be widowed; the others still had their partners, even if badly injured. Her sense of injustice was burning and had no outlet. She grimly did her duty bringing up her two sons, but they keenly felt what a burden they were and what a poor substitute for her husband. One left for a life in Australia as soon as he was an adult. The other stayed and tried to provide support for his mother, but it was never good enough. When he married, his wife then bore the brunt of her mother-in-law's anger and bitterness.

The son's wife was a competent, reasonable woman, but holding down a professional job and bringing up children herself meant that her mother-in-law's constant, cutting criticism and (unjust) implication that the couple were neglecting Mabel took its toll. Mabel's sense of abandonment reached desperation when they proposed a move to Scotland and she sought help. She was surprised when the assessing therapist suggested anger work as well as therapy for her depression.

Road rage

What is it about being in a car that brings out anger? When discussing their anger with group facilitators, mild young professionals with few examples of expression of anger in their normal life would admit to self-righteous rage behind the wheel. There could be two factors at work here. On the one hand, the roads are crowded. People frequently have unrealistic expectations of journey times given the volume of traffic, road works etc. This leads to heightened stress levels as the 'threat' of being late, throwing out one's planned schedule etc., is picked up by the body and translated into a fight/flight response. That focuses the mind on whatever is wrong. Raging about traffic volume is far less satisfying than homing in on the driving deficiencies or disregard of rules of other motorists – that at least gives someone to blame. (In the case of too many cars on the road, you could reasonably be seen as part of the problem – not very satisfying!)

The other factor is the way in which cars separate people. Because you are locked into your own private space, the usual inhibition against yelling at people or attacking them is removed. In the same way that people sing in their cars in a way they would not in a public place, they feel safe to let their anger take over. Mostly this is harmless, apart from resulting in the driver feeling stressed and frazzled. Sometimes, when it leads to actual confrontation, it is not.

The purpose of the reviewing worksheet for this week (if you are following a chapter a week) is to help you to notice how the main themes of this chapter apply in your life.

Reviewing behaviour

Worksheet 3C

Again, notice and write down smaller disturbances – feeling slightly miffed, things getting under your skin, feeling uneasy about something – as well as any major experiences of anger. But this time, note also your reaction to what happened and decide whether your anger was inhibited or disinhibited.

Date and time	What was happening/ what happened	Your reaction	Inhibition or disinhibition

Date and time	What was happening/ what happened	Your reaction	Inhibition or disinhibition

Chapter summary

This is the last chapter of Part 1 of this book, and the last chapter concerned with providing a general understanding of anger and how it operates as an introduction to making changes.

After reading this chapter, you should have an understanding of:

- inhibition and disinhibition
- how these apply to your own situation
- anger and the brain
- anger and alcohol and drugs
- what happens to or can happen to anger that is inhibited.

There is one particularly important message to take from Part 1. That is the recognition that there is no 'boss'. This means that what feels like 'you' wanting to do something could be something else, for instance, your threat system picking up some echo from the past and your body getting ready for action in response to it. If that action is 'fight', it could spell trouble for the real you!

Once you realize this, you are in a position to start the serious business of trying to become the boss – for at least some of the time. Being the boss will not be like being in the driving seat of a car. It will be more like the experience of a surfer in turbulent seas – looking out for and catching a wave, and sometimes being hurled underwater in the process. The rest of the book is about how to do this. Happy surfing!

PART 2

Tackle

Get to grips with what you need to do to make a change

CHAPTER 4

Taking control of your body

Overview

The first three chapters demonstrated what a major part the body plays in unwanted anger reactions. It is the body picking up a sense of threat and getting ready for action that can land us in trouble! Added to that, the sense of threat is often mainly to do with things that happened in the past and out of line with the current situation.

In this chapter we will look in detail at:

- what is going on when this happens
- effective and immediate ways to take charge of the situation
- how to switch your body out of action mode when, as is usually the case, running away or fighting is not a helpful response.

Monitoring your progress

Look back at Worksheet 2B and Worksheet 3C; quickly fill in Worksheet 3C for the last few days if you have not already done so.

Notice what the worksheets tell you in general. Are you getting better at picking up when something has got to you, even if it has not resulted in full-blown anger? Are these times more or less frequent than you would have predicted before you started keeping a log? Is any sort of a pattern emerging – times, places, situations, people that keep cropping up?

Then look at the column about your reaction, in particular your body's reaction. What do you notice in the following areas? Note changes in the table that follows.

Part of the body	Changes noticed when feeling angry
Heart rate	
Breathing	
Muscles: face	
Muscles: shoulders	
Muscles: arms and hands	
Effect on thinking	
Stomach	
Bladder and bowel	
Headache? Any other pain?	
Temperature	
What would others see?	
Other	

Noticing your early warning sign

Did you note something in a lot of the categories? Or not many? There are reasons why people who are prone to anger don't notice what their body is doing, as the case study below of Mick illustrates. However, noticing what is going on is the first step to making changes. Most people can identify the part of their body that picks up a sense of threat first, when they start to think about it. What part of your body is that for you? I notice my shoulders getting tense, or a sinking feeling in my stomach at times like that: for instance, when something is being said – even before it has really dawned on me that what is being said is bad news for me in some way. What do you notice first? This is your 'early warning sign' and recognizing this will be really useful as you start to take charge, to become the 'boss for the day' (remembering that overall there is no boss).

So what is going on when the body decides to get ready for action? Human beings essentially have two modes of operation. The ordinary, everyday, calm 'everything is fine' mode, and the emergency 'action stations' mode. It is as if a switch is flipped and all the different parts of our bodies and minds operate in a different gear, a different mode.

'Action mode' changes to the body and mind

In response to a perceived threat, the following 'action mode' changes take place all over the body.

Change	What happens	Why	What you notice
Heart rate	Speeds up	For vigorous action you need extra blood in all your limbs and organs; the heart achieves this by pumping the blood round faster	Heart thumping Feel hot and sweaty (because that extra blood makes you hot)

Stomach and digestive system	Digestion etc. is switched off	When there is an emergency, resources (blood) need to be withdrawn from the less essential parts of the body to the parts that are vital for survival	Varies, but often includes: 'butterflies' – an uncomfortable feeling in the stomach feeling sick needing the toilet
Breathing	Rapid, shallow Breathe in fast; breathe out less	When you engage in vigorous action, you need plenty of oxygen, and you use it up quickly, hence gulping in air in fast, short breaths	If (as is likely) you are not engaging in vigorous action, this sort of breathing soon feels uncomfortable It affects the ability to think normally (below) You could start to feel as if you cannot breathe, which is frightening; if it continues, it can lead to panic
Muscles	Become tense	Extra blood and oxygen is sent to the muscles so that your legs can run away fast or your arms fight effectively	Feel tense, which sometimes leads to shaking and tremor in the limbs, and pain if prolonged Tension in the head and face muscles leads to headache

(*Continued*)

Change	What happens	Why	What you notice
Thinking	Becomes focused on threat (tunnel vision), fails to take in the bigger picture; if prolonged, leads to confusion	If you are in real danger, you need to concentrate on coping with that. The change in your breathing disturbs the balance between oxygen and carbon dioxide in the brain, as a result of breathing for action without using that extra oxygen and not breathing out enough. If this continues, the brain cannot cope and panic and confusion result	

Action mode and thinking

These changes to the body are uncomfortable and are designed to get you moving. It is the effect on your thinking that can get you locked into a vicious circle. This can be hard to escape. It is the 'tunnel vision' mentioned in the table above.

As far as your body is concerned, there is an immediate threat that you must deal with if you are to survive (e.g. a sabre-toothed tiger). Thinking needs to focus on threat and ignore any wider thoughts. However, when there is not an obvious physical threat to deal with – probably the case in most of the situations you have logged on your worksheet (any tigers this week? I thought not …) – the mind looks around for what the threat might be. If you start looking for threat … you will find it! At this point, the Emotion compartment of the mind takes charge. Remember, this part of the brain does not 'do' time, and will helpfully suggest plenty of examples of threat from the past, as well as coming up with possible future dangers. By now, things are starting to look serious, so the body responds by stepping up its 'action mode' preparations – and driving your thinking deeper into tunnel vision. This is how anger takes over and people say and do things they later regret.

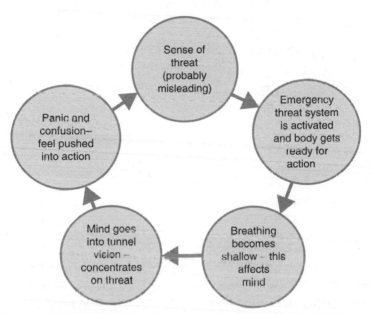

Figure 4.1: A threat vicious circle

Dealing with action mode

It should be clear by now that the key to taking charge of your anger reaction is to pick up the switch to action mode in time (those early warning signs) and switch it off *before* you do something you will regret.

Going down the list of physical changes, you will notice a number that you have no control over – have you tried slowing your heart rate or getting your digestive system back on track? Luckily, there are two over which you have a lot of conscious control: muscle tension and breathing. Controlling muscle tension can be achieved with relaxation exercises, which are very useful. You can get an audio guide to learning how to relax on CD or MP3. Relaxation exercises have a real place in the sort of lifestyle changes we will talk about in Chapter 9. In an emergency, however, muscle relaxation is not the place to start: breathing is.

Hyperventilation

When the body gets ready for action, it automatically gulps in as much air as it can, as quickly as possible. This does not leave much time for breathing out. Where strenuous physical activity follows (as in a real fight with or flight from a sabre-toothed tiger), this extra oxygen will be used up in enabling the body to sustain vigorous action. In the absence of vigorous action, the extra breathing in has an unbalancing effect on the chemicals that control the blood supply to the brain. This is part of the 'tunnel vision' effect on the mind. It helps to shut down the sort of wider considerations that would advise caution and would enable you to sort out past from present. It is not a healthy or sustainable state, and leads to sensations of confusion and panic if allowed to continue.

As hyperventilation results from breathing in too much, the obvious correction is to breathe out more, as suggested in the exercise below.

Doing something about the breathing is a real help, as it signals to the body that action mode is not needed, and reverses the 'tunnel vision' vicious circle that can easily lock someone into an anger response. In order to help your breathing, the first necessity is to be able to step back, and even to literally leave the situation – step out of the room if you can make a plausible excuse or if you have discussed with those close to you that this is the best course of action at such times. This gives you the space to take charge of your breathing. When this is not possible (e.g. you are talking to your boss at work), a good alternative is the traditional counting up to ten under your breath. (Further techniques of mindfulness and grounding will be introduced in Chapter 5).

It must be stressed that this advice is for the purpose of taking control in the moment; avoidance is *not* a desirable long-term strategy! Once you have gained the necessary thinking space to enable you to do something about your breathing, try the relaxation breathing exercise that follows the case study.

Case study: Jason and Gill

Jason and his wife Gill were similar in character. They both had lively tempers, and early in their relationship a good row had added spice. Now, with three small children and job worries, Jason recognized that their arguments were getting out of hand. He was desperate not to resort to violence. A couple of times he had pushed Gill in the course of an argument. On one of those occasions, she had stumbled and cut her face as a result. Jason felt terribly guilty for having attacked a woman and also frightened of what could happen next. Even before starting the anger management course, he tried to leave the house when he realized an argument was getting out of hand. He knew that if he could walk around the block, even if it was dark and raining, he would get his head back together and he could calm things down. Yes, there was also the temptation to pop into the local pub and have a pint, maybe more if his mates were there …

The trouble was, by the time it got to that stage, Gill had reached 'action mode' too and she was determined not to let him go out. To some extent, this was understandable, as she had been left wondering where he was and in charge of the kids so unable to follow (this was the 1990s, so before the days of mobile phones). But also, in the heat of the moment, the most important thing for her was to win the argument, which she could not do if Jason left.

The solution was a joint interview as part of the pre-group assessment process, when Jason and Gill were able to discuss their arguments at a time when they were calm and in the presence of the therapist, a third party. Gill agreed that Jason must be allowed to leave the house when things were getting heated. Jason undertook to be gone no longer than half an hour and on no account to go to the pub.

Relaxation breathing

As 'action mode' breathing means you breathe in more than you breathe out, all you have to do to switch off your threat system is … breathe out more than you breathe in!

A bonus is that as you breathe in, you naturally tense your chest muscles, and then you naturally relax them on the out-breath. So it is very easy to concentrate on relaxing your muscles on the out-breath!

The trick is to keep practising this so that it is easy to do when under stress. Practice is key. Practise this breathing at odd moments. Start practising when you are quite relaxed; it will not work if you start straight away at times when you are very tense. Get good at it, and then you can expect it to work for you when you need it.

Build some regular check-in times into your day to practise the breathing, and use it when you want to get to sleep!

Practical advice ⇨

Relaxation breathing

Breathe out more than you breathe in!

- Breathe IN for a count of 1
- Breathe OUT for a count of 2

And you do not need to breathe in immediately after you have breathed out; you can have a short rest.

- Breathe IN for a count of 1
- Breathe OUT for a count of 2
- and R-E-S-T

As you naturally relax your chest muscles on the out-breath, it is very easy to relax your muscles on the out-breath!

- Breathe IN
- and R-E-L-A-X

Keep practising this so that it is easy to do when you really need it.

Breathing will reduce anxiety if you catch it early; notice what your body is telling you – pick up your first signs of anxiety, and then lengthen your breathing.

This breathing should help you to think more clearly.

Other breathing methods

You might have come across breathing methods used as a way of calming down. The popularity of yoga has led to greater awareness of breathing and a considerable body of knowledge about breathing, based on an ancient practice. A lot of yoga breathings require you to count up to more than two, and to do other things, like closing alternate nostrils. Also, you might be instructed to hold your breath. A popular form of breathing, known as square breathing, incorporates holding the breath for the same count as the in breath and the out-breath.

All these breathing methods have their place within the discipline and practice of yoga, but they do not translate so well to the task of switching off 'action mode'. There are two reasons for this:

- the methods require a degree of calm concentration, present in the attendees at a yoga class but absent when the fight/flight action response is getting into gear and the mind has gone into tunnel vision; action breathing feels like the right thing to do, so you are likely to reverse something complicated like a 7 in–11 out breathing pattern to a 11 in–7 out breathing pattern and make things worse!
- the methods might incorporate breath holding. When you are in action mode, and instructed to hold your breath, this will feel absolutely right. The trouble is, it will feel so right that you will carry on holding it and forget to breathe out!

So relaxation breathing can be the key to switching out of 'action mode' and tunnel vision and into a mode where you can see the bigger picture and the wider consequences. It must be emphasized that this is a strategy to buy you time. It is only the beginning of anger management – there is a lot more to that before you really start to make your anger work for you rather than against you. If leaving the situation and using breathing is all you are doing, you will be missing out on dealing with the situations that have produced the anger in the first place. However, it is a crucial first step. It is the foundation. It should never be forgotten or lightly dismissed.

Case study: Mick (2)

Mick was a big man; pleasant and mild most of the time, until, he claimed, he would suddenly switch and go ballistic – with no warning. He followed the first few sessions of the anger management group with great attention. He did not come back with written homework, but the examples he gave showed that he had been giving the programme serious thought in the week in between sessions. In particular, he was using the breathing to great effect.

He reported that at the regular Friday get-together of the crew from work in the pub he had noted that he was starting to feel tense. He used the breathing technique and as a result, instead of rising to the bait and flying off the handle at what colleagues were saying, as he usually did, he saw the bigger picture; they were deliberately winding him up. Watching Mick blow his top was their regular Friday entertainment. He used the breathing to stay calm and not rise to the bait. He watched with some satisfaction as they started to look silly instead of him.

Mick related his triumph at the next group, where it made a big impression. He said that he now realized that when he thought his anger rose from nothing to red-hot in no time, it was because he was missing the stages in between. He was missing them because of a habit of not attending to anything disturbing: maintaining his persona as the cool guy, unaffected by things. Noticing how his body was reacting and dealing with the changes before he lost his temper was the key to taking charge of his anger.

Monitoring and the process of change

This chapter's worksheet invites you to notice when something gets to you, how your body reacts and how you cope.

A note on the process of change. We are probably talking here about breaking deeply ingrained habits. It is unrealistic to expect this to happen overnight. Expect a process, which goes as follows.

1 You note that you lost your temper as usual and did not notice anything beforehand – it crept up on you. Try thinking back; were there any signs of your body getting ready for action that you missed?

2 You note that you have almost reached the anger 'point of no return' before losing your temper, but it is too late to stop it. Congratulate yourself that you noticed! You are making progress!

3 Maybe you notice when something fairly unimportant bothers you – a flutter in the stomach, a bit of tension. You weren't going to lose your temper over it, but you did notice that something had got to you. Excellent! Really congratulate yourself! We are getting somewhere!

4 Maybe you notice your body tensing etc. and try relaxation breathing, but the anger has already got too much of a hold. Again, congratulate yourself. You are on your way.

5 Maybe next time, you notice in good time what your body is up to. You use the breathing or make an excuse to give yourself space. You have time to think up a really smart, but not cutting response. You are now truly on the road towards managing your anger.

Reviewing behaviour

Worksheet 4A

Use the table below to note when something got to you, what it was, how your body reacted and how you coped.

Date and time	What was happening/ what happened	Body reaction	How you coped

Chapter summary

After reading this chapter you should now:

- understand the changes that take place when your body switches into 'action mode'
- know why these changes take place
- start to notice these changes, picking up your 'early warning signs'
- have learned a simple relaxation breathing exercise to help switch off 'action mode' so that you can think clearly and decide what to do
- have started to practise this breathing exercise regularly
- be monitoring the times when something gets to you, even if this is not proper anger, and noting these on your worksheet
- have started to use breathing and giving yourself space as an immediate coping strategy.

We have covered a lot already but this is where things start to get serious!

CHAPTER 5

Now you have a choice!

Overview

In this chapter we reach the point where you have the means to control your body's immediate push to action. This means that you have a choice.

- We explore what you can choose and the consequences
- We consider the challenge of accepting that you have that amount of control
- Mindfulness in introduced as another tool for managing anger.

Monitoring your progress

Look at Worksheet 4A from Chapter 4. Fill it in now if you haven't already. What have you noticed about the way in which your body reacts to something that makes you feel angry or to some sort of a sense of threat?

Did you learn anything by starting to notice that? Often people don't track the build-up of tension because they don't want to be angry. However, there are advantages to paying attention to what your body is telling you:

- The physical reaction is telling you that something is wrong. It is in your interests to know that so that you can decide what needs to be done.
- If you notice your stress reaction early enough, you will be able to do something about it effectively before it gets out of hand.

This is at the heart of anger management. Moral: keep monitoring.

Also, did you manage to do something to take control of your reaction? Or think about what you might have done if you missed the opportunity? Whichever it was, congratulate yourself – look back at the list of stages in the process of change in Chapter 4. From this you will see that, even if you missed the moment this time, if you are starting to be aware, you are on the road!

Choices and consequences

To continue the road metaphor, you have now reached an important crossroads. By taking control of your immediate anger reaction and learning to switch out of your body's action mode, you can now think

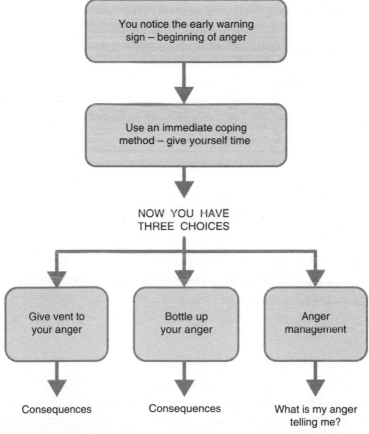

Figure 5.1: Choices

53

clearly. This means that *you* can decide what to do. Up to now, your body would have taken over and made the decisions for you. You are now in a powerful position.

- You can, if you choose, allow the anger to take its course. You can let them have it (whatever that means in the particular context).
- You can hang onto your anger, keep it in, bottle it up.
- Or you can choose to manage your anger so that you can learn from it (remember, it is telling you that something is wrong – you need to know about that) and put its energy to good use (remember the 'Anger and electricity' section in Chapter 1?).

Consequences list

Worksheet 5A

Think of either a time recently when you felt angry or a common anger situation for you. Thinking about that event or situation, consider what the consequences might be of each of the three possible choices. Note down the consequences in the table below.

Consequences of giving vent to your anger	Consequences of bottling up your anger	Consequences of managing your anger

What did you notice doing that exercise? It was a central exercise for the anger management programme I ran. Each time a group did it, what always emerged was that there were pluses and minuses for each of the columns (but overall the minuses, the downside, won out for the first two columns). What follows is a typical result of asking the group.

Consequences of giving vent to your anger	Consequences of bottling up your anger	Consequences of managing your anger
Violence; someone gets hurt	Feel stressed	Feel good about yourself – in control
Look silly – lose respect	Doesn't solve anything	Look better in front of others; respect
Lose relationships	Can be bad for your health	Use the anger constructively
Feel better – get it out	Might all come out at once later	Good for keeping relationships
Get it across – they know how you feel	Might go away	Good for reputation at work
Trouble with the police	Might not be worth bothering about	No problems with the law

Was your list similar? If it was very different, think about it – interesting!

So, the usual conclusion is that once you are in control and have the choice, managing your anger is on balance the best way to go. However, for many people two major obstacles crop up at this point. We will deal with them one at a time.

Obstacle 1: Do you want to have a choice?

Session five of the group, the Choices session, was crunch time for a lot of the participants. Even if they personally had not got anywhere with the breathing exercise, usually one or more of the other members had – like Mick in the case study in Chapter 4.

We have already looked at the way in which people come to anger management with different degrees of personal commitment to working on change. Often there is pressure from others (wife, husband, boss etc.) or from circumstances (might lose partner, children, job, liberty etc.) pushing people to seek this help. It is natural for people to waver. After a particularly narrow escape from one of the potential losses, they might be absolutely determined. Then, when things have settled down and gone back to normal, the idea of managing life without using the threat of losing their temper starts to look rather challenging. The attitude can subtly change. It can settle down to a sort of gamble as follows:

- 'Need to give it a go to keep everyone happy.'
- 'It might work – that would be good!'
- 'On the other hand, it looks a bit feeble … Unlikely to work.'
- 'That might be even better …'

It was usually the Choices session at which it became apparent to group members that anger management was likely to work. That was invariably the point at which some people left.

Also, there was often another dynamic within the group that led some people to leave at about that point; the same issue is unlikely to be a problem for one person reading a book (but you never know). The problem arises because we are dealing with human beings. Human beings often want to be right, to be in control. Angry human beings are used to getting their own way, being looked up to.

Social hierarchy

Research into the role and importance of social hierarchy is undertaken by a school of psychology known as evolutionary psychology. These psychologists start from an acute awareness of the evolutionary journey travelled by human beings. This has taken us from slime in the sea to where we are today, but the great ape stage is particularly interesting in shedding light on our social behaviour. Research suggests that whatever socially acceptable reasons our sophisticated new brains supply after the event, our behaviour is actually driven by where we judge ourselves to be in the social pecking order (an image taken from chickens) or primate hierarchy, and how we manage this.

Think of the clash of 'alpha males' in a board meeting. This is an example of positions in the primate hierarchy being established. Relevant to anger management is the way that establishing this takes place below the radar of our conscious minds. When our position in the hierarchy is threatened, we first pick up the news in our gut; our bodies. We sense fear or anger, and this influences what we do next. Conscious thought lags behind. Using this model, Paul Gilbert, in his interesting book on depression (Gilbert, 1992), poses and answers the question: 'What is the function of depression?' His answer makes sense from an evolutionary persepctive.

If you get the impression that you are at the bottom of the primate hierarchy, the only safe course of action is to withdraw, stop competing and shut down physically. This neatly explains the characteristics of depression: both the physical effects and the thinking style designed to keep an individual down. For angry people, the same logic explains why it can sometimes be so hard to let go, to withdraw gracefully, to concede that someone else has a point. That would be to give up that precious position in the primate hierarchy!

So, it tended to be the Choices session when the question of dominance in the group arose. Who was in charge? A particular group member or the facilitators? Who was top dog? The conformist or the rebel? If someone is used to getting their own way by using anger, knuckling under can feel like a step too far; see the case study of Josh below.

Case study: Josh (2)

Josh came to the Choices group session pretty wired. He had just handled a really good batch of coke and had had his fair share of it. Of course, he had assured the therapist who assessed him before joining the course that he was going to abstain, but that was simply not possible. These people didn't live in the real world ...

At the group, everyone was all over Mick after his triumph using the breathing exercise to wrongfoot his mates at the pub. Josh felt excluded and outraged – at the previous session he had loudly denounced the breathing exercise as silly in the face of his serious anger problem. Clearly no one took any notice of him.

Then the facilitator made the point that by using an immediate strategy like stepping away and/or breathing, you would have a choice about losing your temper. Josh just could not let that go. No one understood his anger. He didn't have a choice. It just took over. He started to express this view loudly and at length. The facilitator, a young woman, cut in calmly, thanking him for his contribution but politely and firmly saying that they needed to move on as there was a lot to cover. Josh shut up for the rest of the session. He didn't come again. He told a disappointed Carmen that it was useless, but in fact it had felt all too useful and likely to work. He just was not used to being sidelined; to not being the one to be looked up to and respected.

Obstacle 2: Is it really that easy?

Stopping a well-oiled, well-practised anger reaction in its tracks is not necessarily that easy. Once the body has gone into action mode, you might be well on your way to action by the time you realize that you need to take charge. I have already suggested leaving the situation and using the breathing exercise as ways to do this. However, there are some situations that you cannot get out of that easily. Or you might not want to leave. Think of Jason and Gill; she did not want him to go as she wanted to finish the argument (and win it). Things might have gone too far for you to take control of your breathing.

Luckily, there is another powerful skill to help you take charge. This one has been developed and introduced into the therapy repertoire since the days when I was running the anger management programme, so it was not included in that. Now, however, it is at the heart of all therapy work that I do with people with varying problems, including anger. I am talking about something that sounds even more ridiculously simple and weak than the breathing exercise, but which is, like the breathing, surprisingly effective: namely, bringing yourself into the present and just noticing – in other words, mindfulness.

What is mindfulness?

Mindfulness is being aware, in the present, and letting go of judgements.

- **What do you do?** You just notice.
- **How do you do it?** This is important. You do it with curiosity, very gently, very compassionately.
- **How long do you do it for?** How long is a piece of string? A minute or two of mindfulness can achieve an enormous amount (and it can feel like an awfully long time too). Serious mindfulness practitioners do it for hours, days, months, years on end, although that is not the sort of thing we are talking about here. There is a whole world of mindfulness. This is just dipping a toe in. But it is powerful stuff, so even just a toe can be extremely helpful.
- **Why do you do it?** Because it is the best way to:
  - ▶ get the emotional and the reasonable parts of the mind working together
  - ▶ bring you into the present – where you can take charge and decide what to do
  - ▶ become, however fleetingly, the 'boss' (remembering that there is no permanent boss).

It sounds straightforward. Why is so much made of it?

Well, it is simple but difficult. It means getting your mind to do something it is not used to doing in two very particular ways as follows:

Past and present

Your mind spends most of its time either in the past, going over what has happened, or in the future, thinking about what might happen. In mindfulness, you cannot stop your mind doing this, nor should you try to. However, you are constantly and gently noticing where it has gone and bringing it back from wandering into the past or the future, to focus on the present.

Judgements

A central discipline in mindfulness is to note and let go of judgements. This is the opposite of what our minds normally do. Our minds are programmed to sort things out – good and bad; me and not me; interesting and boring – and to go with the option we judge best. Like past and future, it is impossible to stop your mind from attempting this sorting, nor should you try. Just notice with gentle and slightly indulgent curiosity what your mind is up to, let the judgements go, and come back to just noticing what is, in the present.

Practical advice ⇨

How do you do it? Like this.

Noticing practice

We are going to introduce this with some simple noticing practice. Although mindfulness is often done with the eyes closed, for this exercise keep them open.

- Turn your attention away from your thoughts to your body.
- Notice how your body feels.
- Notice your weight on the chair, floor etc.
- Notice your feet on the floor.
- Notice the things you normally do not notice because they are not important.
- Our minds naturally judge things all the time – interesting/not interesting etc. In this exercise, just notice those judgements, gently let go of them and take in everything.
- Notice any areas of tension, pain etc. and then let your attention move away from them.
- Notice your spine holding up your body.

- Notice your head at the top of your spine.
- Lift your head and look around.
- Notice something in this room that you've never noticed before, probably because it was not important.
- Notice what you can hear – again, notice any judgements and just let them go.
- Notice the fact that you are breathing.
- Notice what that feels like.

This is the first step towards mindfulness – grounding yourself in the present, using your senses to stop your mind going off in all directions. In later chapters, we will go further into mindfulness in order to use it to notice and step back from persistent thoughts, for instance.

If you can practise this sort of noticing regularly, just for a few minutes at a time, you will be in a much better position to bring yourself into the present and *really* decide what to do when you notice your body getting ready for action. You will be able to choose.

Behaviour changing strategy

Worksheet 5B

Use this mindfulness practice chart to help bring mindfulness into your daily life. Enter when you managed a brief mindfulness session: how long did it last; what did you notice?

	Morning	Afternoon	Evening
Monday			
Tuesday			

	Morning	Afternoon	Evening
Wednesday			
Thursday			
Friday			
Saturday			
Sunday			

Evidence base for mindfulness

You might reasonably ask: 'What has ancient Buddhist practice to do with me in the 21st century?' The answer is that it has been proved, by rigorous research trials, that it is a really useful technique in an increasing number of circumstances. These randomized controlled trials (RCTs) compare people who have undertaken a course of mindfulness with those that have not.

It all started with Jon Kabat-Zinn. He applied his Buddhist practice to helping large classes of ordinary people with problems of stress and pain, to stunning effect. Importantly, he also researched the outcomes he was getting and published these. He has written very accessibly about this in his book *Full Catastrophe Living*, a title taken from *Zorba the Greek* (Kabat-Zinn, 1996). His approach was quickly taken up by others. Segal, Williams and Teasdale used mindfulness to help prevent relapse in depression through mindfulness based cognitive therapy (MBCT), and also demonstrated its usefulness through research (Williams et al., 2007; Segal et al., 2002). Marsha Linehan made it the centrepiece of her therapy for people who self-harm, attempt suicide and engage in other chaotic behaviour (a collection unhelpfully called borderline personality disorder). Her therapy, dialectical behaviour therapy (DBT), is described in Chapter 2 (Linehan, 1993). Again, she collected the evidence. As a result, both MBCT and DBT feature in the National Institute for Health and Care Excellence (NICE) guidelines and so are recommended for people with these problems seeking NHS help. I have trained in both these approaches to mindfulness, but am more influenced by the way in which it is applied in DBT.

Mindfulness has also been used to help people with psychosis, obsessive–compulsive disorder, alcohol and drug problems, stress, pain and depression, and evaluated to show its usefulness – so why not anger? And that is just mental health. Schools, businesses and even parliament see a use for this technique to bring people back into the present moment and allow them to choose where to put their attention. I recommend it!

So the grounding effect of being aware in the moment, the beginning of mindfulness, can be added to breathing and taking space in order to choose what to do with your anger. The next case study presents someone who found the idea of making a choice, which means being mindful, really useful.

Case study: Bev (1)

Bev faced life as if a battle, experiencing the world as a hostile place. It was easy to see how this was the result of her Emotion Mind serving up a past situation as if it was in the present. Senior school for Bev had been sheer hell. A bad choice of 'friend' to confide in, combined with a stocky, brush-haired appearance, led to an early outing of her gay sexual orientation. This resulted in rejection and cruel taunts from the girls and serious sexual harassment from the boys. Understandably, her school attendance was patchy and she left early.

She used her considerable physical strength, and need for release of tension, to throw herself into manual work. However, her sharp intelligence, particularly with figures, shone through, and she found herself in an office behind a computer, with more money and status but no outlet for her frustration. She would hold it together at work for a while, before the next furious outburst. Her job was at risk. She took advice and joined the anger management programme.

The problem was that her body would quickly take over. She would misinterpret innocent remarks at work and fly off the handle. Her boss had taken her aside on a couple of occasions and managed to get across to her that she was being unreasonable, leading to her joining the group. The trouble was, it was really hard to break the habit and Bev was getting worried that being angry all the time was just who she was and that there was nothing she could do about it.

The idea of taking control, of having a choice really struck a chord with her: an 'Aha' moment. As she was quite confident, leaving the situation – going for a break rather than sticking in there and letting things escalate – was something she could manage. And it made her feel good that if she decided, on reflection, that the other party was out of order she could still let them have it!

The time has come to try out the idea of using an immediate coping strategy to give you the opportunity for choice, and to make that choice, in your own life. Here is a worksheet to help you with this.

Reviewing behaviour

Worksheet 5C

Use the table below to note when something got to you, what was happening, how you coped immediately (breathing? mindfulness?) and what choice you made.

Date and time	What was happening	Immediate coping method	What choice?

Chapter summary

After reading this chapter, you have learned about:

- the choices you can make once you have noticed the beginnings of anger and done something about it
- the challenges that this can pose
- applying brief, grounding mindfulness to enable you to take control in the present
- practising this mindfulness regularly, at odd moments throughout the day.

CHAPTER 6

Using choice wisely

Overview

This chapter covers what happens next, after you have bought yourself time and the ability to choose by using an immediate coping strategy.

Depending on the answers to questions posed in this chapter, you might:

- use problem-solving to resolve the situation that has made you angry
- discharge your anger safely and productively.

This chapter will take you through how to use both of these approaches.

Monitoring your progress

I hope you have been monitoring the times when you felt angry, or just felt things getting to you, and what you have started to do about this. Look at Worksheet 5C from Chapter 5 (or think over the week and fill it in now – better late than never!). Do you notice anything? How are you doing with bringing in new strategies? How are you managing with taking control?

Don't worry if you are still losing your temper. There is still a lot of ground to cover. Remember, you have had a lot of practice doing things the old way. It is not surprising if things don't change overnight. If you really want them to change, they will!

Also, how have you got on with bringing some simple, grounding mindfulness into your life? How has your practice at noticing things in the present gone? What have you noticed there?

Managing the anger – first step

The first step to actually managing your anger (as opposed to just stopping it in its tracks) is to ask it a question. Your anger is trying to tell you something. It is trying to tell you that something is wrong. If you simply blunder into action at that point, you will never have the opportunity to ask the crucial question 'What is wrong?'. After all, once you know that, it might be possible to put it right. This chapter introduces a technique to put matters right, if that is realistic, using the method of problem-solving. All the valuable energy that your anger has mobilized by getting your body ready for action can then be put into the important work of reaching a solution.

Equally, whatever is wrong might be something that you cannot put right just like that. You cannot expect your anger to just go away. Learning how to discharge anger safely and productively is just as crucial to anger management.

Time to introduce another diagram to help you to navigate your way through the answer that your anger gives you when you ask it the question 'Why anger?'.

Self-assessment

We are going to apply Figure 6.1 to one or more of your examples.

Look at your Worksheet 5C, or note down a recent time when you felt angry if you have not done so already on the worksheet. Now take that example and work through the process in Figure 6.1, filling in Worksheet 6A.

Worksheet 6A

You noted that you were experiencing anger, or the beginnings of anger. Maybe you noticed tension in your body, e.g. a feeling in the stomach, or angry thoughts – a sense of being under threat.

This means that your body is picking up that something is wrong. It is important that you know about that. Often it is easier to tackle something straight away rather than let it build up into a major issue.

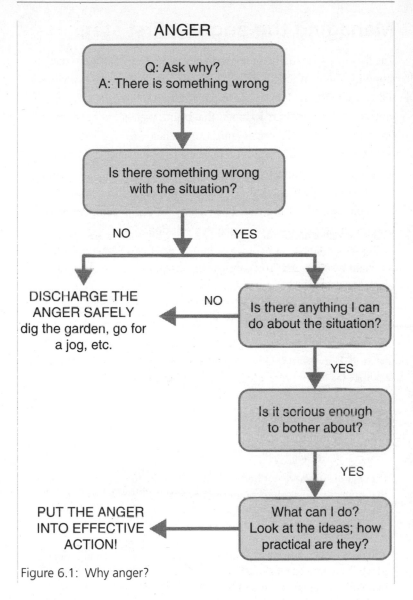

Figure 6.1: Why anger?

Q1 Is there something wrong about the situation? (What is the situation?)

_____

_____

_____

If the answer to Q1 is yes:

Q2 Is there something I can do about the situation? (*Circle one answer.*)
YES / NO

Q3 Is it important enough to be worth bothering about or should I let it go? (*Circle one answer.*)
YES / NO

If yes, use the example in Figure 6.1 to work through the problem-solving section that follows.

If you answered No to Q1, use the work on thinking in Chapter 7 to help you get to the bottom of what got you so wound up.

If you answered No to Q2, use the section on discharging anger later in this chapter to help you.

I hope that Worksheet 6A has helped you to take your anger reaction seriously (as it deserves) and to work out where to go next with it.

Problem-solving

Problem-solving is a widely used technique in counselling and other contexts. A useful website with more information can be found at www.problemsolvingtherapy.ac.nz. Problem-solving might seem simple and obvious at first glance: you look at the problem logically, go through the options, looking at each critically, choose the best one and put it into action. The trouble is that human beings are not naturally logical. As with mindfulness, you have to discipline yourself to actually go through the procedure. Here is a guide to how to do this.

1 You need to be in a reasonable frame of mind; emotions get in the way if you are trying to be logical.

2 You have to switch off your mind's usual way of working, which is to take short cuts. Our brain is actually designed not to think things through from first principles every time, but instead to come up with an answer quickly; this is known as 'heuristic' thinking. Inevitably, the answer that heuristic thinking produces is governed by what we usually do, our prejudices etc. This is handy in everyday life – we don't want to spend ages on every little decision – but it is a barrier to coming up with new solutions to problems. If you always do what you always did, you will always get what you always got!

3 You need to specify everything very clearly. If you are fuzzy about what the problem is and where you want to get to in terms of a solution, you will never find an effective new solution that you can carry out.

Worksheet 6B is a problem-solving worksheet that you can work through using an example of anger. The sort of anger situation you need for this exercise is one where you have identified that the anger was both justified and worth doing something.

Behaviour changing strategy ♘

Worksheet 6B: Problem-solving

Describe the problem (make this clear and specific).

_____

_____

How will things be different when the problem is solved (again, be very specific)?

_____

_____

Now brainstorm possible solutions to the problem, giving also the advantages (pros) and disadvantages (cons) of each possible solution.

Add a rating between 0 and 10 for each possible solution, where 10 = a brilliant idea and 0 = a non-starter.

Suggested solution	Pros	Cons	Rating

Now develop an action plan to deal with the problem, using the solutions that you think are the best ideas. You need to be specific about the solution and the steps you are going to take to achieve it. You should also set a deadline for taking each step.

Solution	Step 1	When by?	Step 2	When by?

To help you work out how to fill in the worksheet, look at the case of Ken and how he used the worksheet to solve his problem.

Case study: Ken (1)

Ken was angry with his former partner. His son Jack (aged 5) did not want to spend access weekends with him and Ken blamed his ex for turning the boy against him. He also blamed having to pay her child support for using up all his money. Looking at the problem objectively, with a bit of help from others in the group, Ken realized that Jack's reluctance to spend the weekend with him was more to do with the fact that all Jack's toys and friends were at his mother's home and they did fun things at the weekend there, whereas at Ken's place all that was on offer was TV. See how he worked through problem-solving process in his worksheet.

Ken's problem-solving worksheet 6B

Describe the problem (make this clear and specific).
Time spent with me needs to be much more fun for Jack. This needs to be managed with limited money.

How will things be different when the problem is solved (again, be very specific)?
Jack will have a good time when he spends the weekend with me and will want to come again next time.

Now brainstorm possible solutions to the problem, giving also the advantages (pros) and disadvantages (cons) of each possible solution.

Add a rating between 0 and 10 for each possible solution, where 10 = a brilliant idea and 0 = a non-starter.

Suggested solution	Pros	Cons	Rating
Work more overtime	Simplest way to earn more money	Hate the job! Exhausted when get home	5
Steal it	Money for treats	It's wrong Probably get caught – more trouble Too scared	2

(Continued)

Suggested solution	Pros	Cons	Rating
Spend less money; budget carefully, spend less in the pub	It would be possible to save a bit that way and be able to do more	Hard work Have to watch the pennies	7
Win the lottery	Great!!!	Unlikely	3
Investigate interesting playgrounds not too far away	Jack would enjoy that Other children there Cheap – just the bus fare	Might rain Bit boring for me	8
Find another parent to go to the park etc. with	Fun for Jack Could be company for me	Don't know where to start Scared to ask people	5
Go to the big library in the middle of town	Could look at picture books, read to him Might be activities – look at the notice board Dry in the rain Free	Bit boring and quite hard work for me	7
Go fishing	Good. Be able to sit still while Jack runs around and explores Other fishermen there with family	Got to get some rods etc., which costs money Rain	9

Now develop an action plan to deal with the problem, using the solutions that you think are the best ideas. You need to be specific about the solution and the steps you are going to take to achieve it. You should also set a deadline for taking each step.

Solution	Step 1	When by?	Step 2	When by?
Plan a fishing trip at the local fishing pond (free)	Look for affordable rods etc. or on a freecycling website	By Friday	Take Jack fishing	Next visit with fine weather
Investigate interesting sounding playgrounds not too far away	Use the internet and ask people at work Look at a map in the library	Next 2 weeks	Take Jack to the park, with the library as back-up if it is wet	Next visit
Spend less money; budget carefully, spend less in pub	Stop getting take-aways Cook more	Today	Put a limit on pub spending	Friday

Ken reported back at the next group meeting. Getting set up for fishing proved more complicated than he had hoped, but he got some suggestions about playgrounds from people at work – in fact, the conversation led to him joining a work colleague and his two children at one playground. Jack had a great time, despite the fact that it was raining off and on. Only the dads grumbled about getting wet. Jack enjoyed being involved in Ken's rather fumbling attempts to make their tea, instead of the usual take-away. Ken's ex-partner (who did want the access visits to work) reported Jack saying that his dad was 'cool'.

There are a few things to notice here:

- Identifying what 'the situation' really is. At first, Ken thought the problem was that his ex-partner was turning Jack against him and that the child support he had to pay did not leave him enough money to give the boy as good a time as he had with his mother. This would be a challenging situation to do anything about. Discussion helped Ken to recognize that the real problem was that the boy had no fun when he was with his dad. It was possible to do something about that.

- The way the brainstorm turned out. Some of the brainstorm ideas were really wild and impractical. That is actually quite important; brainstorming only works if you are prepared to think outside the box. If you don't allow your imagination to range freely, you will come up with the 'same old, same old' and remain stuck. You can always rule out the impractical ideas at the pros and cons stage. Also, notice that the action plan did not quite work out as planned, but it certainly got things moving.

I am afraid there are no guarantees that problem-solving will always be so successful, but I hope you have got the idea and will give it a go!

Discharging anger

We are now going to look at the other arm of the flow-chart in Figure 6.1 – the one where you answer 'No' to either of the questions.

This means that you are angry, something is wrong, but you cannot do anything about it – not good. This is where discharging anger comes in. This means that not only does the anger not get bottled up and make you stressed and more likely to explode about something small in the future, but also that you can use all the lovely energy of the body in action mode for something that will help you. Remember about anger and electricity in Chapter 1? So we are going to look at discharging anger step by step.

Step 1

Follow the steps on Figure 6.1 as far as 'No', i.e. notice that you are angry. Use an immediate coping strategy, like breathing, to be able to think about it and decide what to do. Review the situation and come to the point where you are angry but either there is nothing you can do about the situation, or it is not really a situation in the present that has sparked your anger.

Step 2

You now have some surplus energy. All you have to do is to choose something to put it into. Choose an activity to put the energy into (carefully).

Choosing an anger discharge activity

Be careful here. If you choose something that encourages you to keep on thinking about what made you angry, the anger will never be discharged – that is because your angry thoughts will keep it alive. What you need is something that takes plenty of energy. Remember: your body is ready for action – you need to give it some or it will stay wound up – but it needs to be something that will take your mind somewhere else. This is the opposite of ways of discharging anger that are often recommended, such as using a punchbag or bashing a pillow. There is scientific evidence to show that such activities can make you more angry rather than less (Bushman, 2002). It is easy to see why that may be, if you think about it. There is nothing interesting in itself about bashing something, so you are likely to carry on thinking about what has made you angry. Thinking about it keeps your anger alive. So much for discharge!

So remember:

- suitable activities need to use energy
- the activities need to help you to move the focus of your thinking from what you are angry about onto something else.

It is easier to do this if you choose something that is rewarding in itself or that you know is useful. Our ancestors probably had an easier time finding a suitable activity in a time when you couldn't keep warm unless you chopped enough firewood, and couldn't wash or cook before you had lugged gallons of water from a well. In modern times, going for a run or going to the gym are often substitutes. There are still physical things that need doing – cleaning the windows or digging the garden for instance. Kneading bread by hand is good too (but not using a bread maker!).

These sorts of activities all help you to direct your thinking away from the anger onto positives. For instance, how much good the run or gym exercise is doing to you, or how much better the windows will look etc.

Step 3

Once you have chosen your activity and are ready to do it, you actually need to drum up a degree of anger. (Does this seem to be the opposite of what I was just saying?) This is to get your body ready for action and give you access to all that energy. This is tricky. You don't want to get so wound up that you lose your temper.

Step 4

When you have got into your chosen activity (and the more absorbing it is the better), let go of thinking about what made you angry. Focus on your activity and the benefits of doing it – whether it is something that is doing you good, like exercise, or something you can enjoy or simply a job that you really need to get out of the way so that you can feel satisfaction over having tackled it.

This is the first step of real anger management.

Expressing anger and creativity

Linked to the topic of discharging anger is the expression of anger. This is another area where caution is vital. In Chapter 5 we looked at how simply giving vent to your anger could be a bad idea. In a worst-case scenario it can lead to violence, but even if it is verbal rather than physical, a shouting match, it tends to lead to people saying hurtful things to each other that they do not really mean. It often leads to an unnecessary dragging-up of the past, as that is how the mind works.

Feelings do need to be expressed, however, and where this can be done in a managed way, expressing the anger can be very beneficial. As with discharging anger, start by checking the initial angry impulse and thinking about it. You might decide that there is something wrong with the situation and that what you need to do about it is to communicate how you feel. In some cases, a simple but forceful expression of feeling that does not get out of control might be very effective. In other cases, it is better to go for a more considered, assertive approach – there is more on assertiveness in Chapter 11. Or you might want to let out the anger on your own. Here you need to choose a spot where you are not going to disturb others or cause more trouble – a howl in the woods or on a windy beach, for instance. You might find that when you think about expressing the anger, what comes out is not rage but tears. Let them flow. Tears are a natural means of expression and healing. They could be the clue to the hurt and pain behind your anger.

Writing the letter that is not sent is another way of getting out how you really feel and facing this without causing endless problems. Yet another effective and positive way of dealing with anger that needs discharging is to express it creatively; there is more on this in Chapter 14.

Behaviour changing strategy ♘

Worksheet 6C: Discharging anger activities

Use this worksheet to list some activities that you could use to discharge your anger. Rate them from 1 to 10 according how much energy they use and how pleasant, useful and creative each one is: 1 = not very much; 10 = a lot.

Activity	Energy use	Pleasure	Usefulness	Creative

Case study: Ken (2)

Another reason why Jack did not like weekends with his father was the room he had to sleep in. It was full of junk from floor to ceiling, apart from the space where his bed went, and it looked as though it had never been decorated. Ken next turned his attention to this. He was still fuming that so much of his money went on child support while he did not really get the benefit of his family, and that he had allowed a potentially good partnership to slip away. Instead of sitting bitterly with all this and a can of beer, on his non-access weekend Ken put that energy into tackling the horrible bedroom. He worked like a fury chucking out stuff – he did not agonize about whether it would be useful, he just put it in a mate's van and they went round to the tip with it. At the tip, he managed to negotiate to bring away a lot of discarded paint for next to nothing (he was starting to get canny about more for less) and also picked up a chair and a desk. He used the rest of the anger energy to scrub the room top to bottom. The next weekend, before it was time to collect Jack, he started painting. He painted everything: floor, ceiling, the old furniture he had bought. The colours were strange and a bit startling, but it all looked nice and clean. Of course, the paint was not dry when he brought Jack back, and the boy had to sleep in the living room, but he was really excited about his new room and impressed with what his dad could do between one weekend visit and the next.

This example shows Ken discharging his anger in a positive way that actually helped to solve the problem, using up surplus energy, being creative – and getting some enjoyment.

Reviewing behaviour

Worksheet 6D

This worksheet invites you to:

- look at situations that have got to you; remember, anything that gets to you is important – it does not need to be full-blown anger
- decide whether these are situations that need problem-solving – in which case, use Worksheet 6B from earlier in the chapter – and/or whether discharging the anger is the best option. Often both are relevant.

Date and time	What is wrong? Is it the situation?	Can you problem-solve it? How?	Discharging the anger – how?

And don't forget to carry on with the mindfulness practice – we will need that in Chapter 7!

Chapter summary

In this chapter you have:

- learned to look at your anger as an important emotion that is telling you something you need to know about
- considered what this is
- worked out whether you can do something about it
- learned a problem-solving protocol to maximize your chances of coming to a good solution
- learned about the safe discharge and expression of anger.

PART 3

Escape

Notice unhelpful thoughts and behaviours and begin to replace them with new ones

CHAPTER 7

Wind-up thinking

Overview

This chapter introduces the important role of thoughts in causing and maintaining anger.

- This is linked to the theory behind cognitive behavioural therapy (CBT).
- The different sorts of anger-causing, or 'wind-up', thoughts are introduced.
- Examples are given of how such thinking has taken over two peoples' lives.
- Mindfulness of thoughts is introduced as a first step to doing something about one's thinking style.

Monitoring your progress

How have you got on with working through your anger, unease or unhappiness about something situations? Any good examples of problem-solving?

Have you managed to try out some good ways of discharging your anger – ways that get you doing things that are good for you, and/or useful, enjoyable etc. – and starting to use the energy of your anger productively?

Keep on with all of that – it is very important – and at the same time take on board the new ways of dealing with anger covered in this chapter.

The role of thoughts in anger

The emphasis so far in this book has been on the role of the body in anger management, and rightly so as it is crucial. However, our thoughts – what we think, and how long we carry on thinking it – are also extremely important. We touched on that in Chapter 6 when explaining how anger management strategies such as hitting a punchbag are counter-productive. This is because they tend to keep us thinking about what has made us angry – and keeping that 'anger thinking' alive is what keeps the anger going.

Our thoughts also play an important role in helping us to understand our anger. Again, we started to consider that by asking 'What is wrong?' in Chapter 6, recognizing that we wouldn't be feeling angry if something was not wrong, and that we need to know what it is! Tracking our thoughts is the way to answer those questions. Ken, for example, was focusing his anger on his ex-partner because he blamed her for turning his son against him (which turned out to be unfair). Recognizing that there might be another reason for his son's unwillingness to visit him was important in finding a solution to that situation. The importance of thoughts in how people cope with how they feel has been fully recognized by cognitive behavioural therapy (CBT), as the following box explains.

Cognitive behavioural therapy

If you try to access psychological therapy on the National Health Service in Britain these days, the likelihood is that you will be offered cognitive behavioural therapy (CBT). This is because research has demonstrated that CBT is helpful to a good proportion of people who try it and that it can be used to address many different problems. Aaron Beck and Albert Ellis were key figures in the 1950s and 1960s who developed what has proved to be an extremely successful therapy (Beck, 1976; Ellis, 1962).

CBT works on the principle that although it is usually how you are feeling that is the problem (e.g. sad, angry, anxious), just trying to feel differently does not change matters. However, there is a close link between feelings, your body's reaction, what you do (which we've been tracking for some chapters in the case of anger) and, crucially for CBT, how you think. For example, a factory is going to close and all the workers have been given notice. Everyone is in exactly the same situation, but think how many different reactions might there be.

- Worker A thinks: 'They have no right to do this. We must fight it.' He contacts the union and proposes a sit-in. He is angry.
- Worker B thinks: 'That is the end for me. No job, no money, no respect. Nowhere to go every day.' He is on the way to depression.
- Worker C thinks: 'At last! I can escape that wretched place! I need to look out for something else, but meanwhile I can do all the things I have been putting off.' He is really happy.

Probably the different reactions had something to do with Workers A, B and C being very different people and having different personal circumstances. However, you can choose how you think – everyone can – and that is crucial for CBT. Worker B might talk to Worker A and cheer up when he decides to join the sit-in. Or he might talk to Worker C and realize that there is an upside to the situation as well as a downside. Classic CBT talks about 'thinking errors' which are to be corrected. The CBT in this book has a slightly different emphasis. Instead of 'maladaptive thinking' that needs to be challenged, it talks of 'unhelpful ways of thinking' and 'wind-up thinking' that needs to be put aside and let go of. This fits well with the idea of mindfulness, introduced in Chapter 5, which we return to in this chapter.

The hot cross bun, or emotion circle

There is a simple diagram that helps you to identify clearly the thoughts etc. behind any anger (or other problem) situation. Greenberger and Padesky, who first devised it, call it a 'hot cross bun' for obvious reasons (Greenberger and Padesky, 1995). It can also be called an emotion circle because it is about unpacking and understanding an emotion.

You can see the emotion circle as a snapshot of your Emotion Mind at the time. Filling in the sections of the Emotion Circle can help you to bring your Reasonable Mind into play.

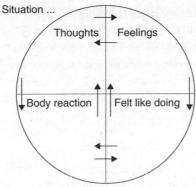

Figure 7.1: The emotion circle. Adapted from Greenberger & Padesky, 2016 (p. 7) with permission of the copyright holder, Christine A. Padesky, www.MindOverMood.com, original copyright 1986.

Reviewing behaviour

Worksheet 7A

Using a copy of Figure 7.1 (see Figure 15.2 for a larger version), think of a recent incident when something got to you (take one from Worksheet 6C, for instance).

- Write a few words to describe the incident that affected your mood (e.g. informed that the factory is going to close).
- Notice how the incident made you feel. Write that in the 'Feelings' section of the circle (e.g. angry, sad, happy).
- Note how your body let you know how you were feeling (e.g. tense if angry, relaxed and energetic if happy etc.) Write that in the 'Body Reaction' section.
- Then remember what thoughts were going through your mind at the time. Write them down in the 'Thoughts' section.
- Now put down what you did or felt like doing in the 'Felt like doing' section.

Does that help you to understand how you reacted? It helps a lot of people to unpack how they respond to things and why something affects them in a particular way. I recommend it whenever you find yourself reacting, particularly if your reaction seems stronger than the situation would warrant or than other people's reactions to it. This is the beginning of starting to understand yourself better.

Wind-up thinking

Now it is time to apply this process to anger. When you get angry, what sorts of phrases occur that you would put in the 'Thoughts' section of the emotion circle? Write down a few of your most commonly used ones.

I am going to guess – one of the following words or phrases cropped up in your list:

- should
- must
- ought
- got to
- always
- never
- 'It's not fair.'

Am I right?

Case study: Mandy and the power of 'It's not fair'

Mandy's whole life was dedicated to getting justice for her disabled daughter. Convinced that her daughter's disabilities were the result of criminal negligence on the part of the hospital that delivered her, she was furious about it and about their refusal to admit this – the hospital claimed her daughter's condition was the result of an unavoidable genetic abnormality. Mandy was even more furious about this claim and about the failure of every medical and judicial avenue she had pursued since; and she had pursued them all, right up to Brussels, in search of the 'justice' she expected. Her search for this justice dominated her and her daughter's life, fuelled by the anger she felt about it and her anger at the deafness of the rest of the world to her cause.

Mandy came to the assessment for therapy session clutching a huge file of legal papers, newspaper cuttings, letters to the queen, prime minister etc., and accompanied by her daughter, who sat quietly in her wheelchair, left out as all her mother's attention was concentrated on the fight. The therapist noted that the quest for justice was maintained by 'It's not fair', and that this way of thinking was keeping anger and a high level of stress permanently on the boil for Mandy, resulting in the effects on her mental health that she was seeking treatment for. The therapist expressed no opinion on the justice of the case, confining herself to pointing out the effects of hanging onto 'It's not fair'.

Mandy was faced with a choice. For anything to change she needed to accept that it was time to let the case go, despite her conviction about its justice; and to start looking forward to life for herself and for her daughter. For Mandy this just felt impossible. Her whole life and identity were bound up with the cause. She had to agree with the therapist that therapy at this time was not for her.

Unhelpful ways of thinking associated with anger

The fact is that once the Emotion Mind takes over, the thinking style changes. CBT has worked out the commonest ways in which this tends to happen. What follows is a list of these emotion-driven styles of thinking, with examples taken from anger.

Shoulds, musts and oughts

These are thoughts that are very hard on ourselves or other people. For example:

- I *ought* to be able to please everybody
- People *should* agree with my point of view

All-or-nothing thinking

This is the thought that if something goes slightly wrong, that's it; you might as well forget the whole thing. For example:

- I cannot get this wallpaper to hang perfectly. I'm going to give up.
- This course hasn't stopped me from losing my temper yet. It is obviously useless. I'm going to leave.

Overgeneralization

This is when one setback is seen as a generalized disaster. Words to watch for are 'always' and 'never'. For example: 'So the meal isn't ready yet.'

- You are *always* late.
- You can *never* organize anything.

Jumping to conclusions

This is when you make assumptions about what other people are thinking (mind-reading) or let your imagination race ahead to what follows on from something that has happened. For example:

- She didn't say 'hello', she must be deliberately ignoring me.
- The boss was in a hurry to get away when I tackled him about my career. He obviously doesn't value me – he probably wants to get rid of me.

You or the world

Either you automatically assume you are the cause of a negative event; for example:

- It must be my fault that those two members have stopped coming to the group. I always thought they didn't like me.

Or you blame everybody else and fail to see what you might have to do with it; for example:

- I couldn't help being late – there's nothing I can do about it if the motorway is clogged up with idiots, and the council chooses now to dig up the road.

A typical argument

Think about how these styles of thinking crop up routinely in your typical argument. You know the scenario. Something has happened *again* to get your anger going and you can feel your body get ready for action. The Emotion Mind takes over and all the examples from the past come flooding in:

'That is absolutely typical of you – saying you have got to go out just when I really need you. You *never* do anything to help around the house. Always sloping off with some excuse. Why can't I ever rely on you to do one little thing for me! Just like that time on our honeymoon when …'

'I can't stand this any longer. Don't you understand, I have got to have some space. Every time I want to go anywhere it is the same story. You just want to keep me prisoner …'

Can you spot some of the emotion-driven thinking styles here? A lot falls into more than one category, but sorting out which is which is not important. The important thing is to become really good at spotting wind-up thinking early so that you can step back and take control before it gets out of hand.

Reviewing behaviour

Worksheet 7B

Look again at the times when you have felt angry recently, when something has got to you. Play the scene back to yourself in your mind. Jot down the thoughts that went through your mind at the time.

_____

_____

_____

_____

_____

Can you spot any of the categories of wind-up thinking in these thoughts?

_____

_____

_____

Then think about afterwards. If something had unsettled you, you probably carried on thinking about it. What phrases stuck in your head?

_____

_____

_____

Again, were any recognizable examples of wind-up thinking?

_____

_____

_____

It is possible to let go of wind-up thinking more easily after the event than in the heat of the moment. Even if you said some things that you need to apologize for, you can do yourself a big favour by letting go of the wind-up thinking once it is all over. That way, even if you have rather a short fuse, anger will not take over your life. The case of Neville illustrates how wind-up thinking can come to take over someone's life – and take it in a very unpromising direction!

Case study: Neville and 'It's their fault'

Neville knew exactly what was wrong with the situation. Having been born into a wealthy family, attended prestigious schools and a prestigious university, and settled into a career with the law department of a prestigious multinational company, he was not short of self-confidence. The problem, according to Neville, was a society overdosing on political correctness.

An angry man at the best of times, the situation he now found himself in was bad enough to really fuel his rage. Following accusations of bullying and harassment from a brave subordinate at work, a host of other fellow employees came forward with instances of his hectoring management style, laced with sexist and racist remarks. They had been putting up with this from Neville for a long time.

The firm suspended him pending investigation. His wife chose that moment to announce, from the safe distance of her sister's house, that she was starting divorce proceedings as she was no longer going to stand for his controlling and domineering ways now the children were old enough to leave home. The world had turned against Neville, and as far as he was concerned it was the world's fault: rightful authority was no longer respected; women and people from other cultures (he phrased it differently) were getting uppity and needed taking down a peg; his friends at the golf club all agreed. And to cap it all, occupational health insisted he take an anger management course!

It was clear at assessment that Neville was going to gain nothing from the course unless he was able to look critically at the way in which he was thinking. He needed to recognize that although this way of thinking helped him to continue to feel good about himself – bolstered by his friends – it was not helpful to him in the long run as it was driving his life straight towards a 'car crash' scenario!

Mindfulness and wind-up thinking

It is clear from both the cases described in this chapter that wind-up thinking can be very central for people. In a later chapter we will look into that more deeply, examining the way wind-up thinking can become part of someone's identity. For the moment, we need to look at ways of noticing what is happening early on and pressing the pause button. To repeat a point made earlier, in the heat of the moment wind-up thinking will occur anyway. The important thing is to:

- notice it and recognize it for what it is
- be able to see that it is not the only possible way of thinking.

The skill of mindfulness is extremely useful here.

Practical advice ⇨

Mindfulness of thoughts: further noticing practice

Start with the same sort of simple noticing practice that was introduced in Chapter 5.

- Turn your attention away from your thoughts to your body.
- Notice how your body feels.
- Notice your weight on the chair, floor etc.
- Notice your feet on the floor.
- Notice something you can see in the room that you've never noticed before – probably because it is not important.
- Notice what you can hear – notice any judgements and just let them go.
- Notice the fact that you are breathing.
- Notice what that feels like.
- Keeping your attention in the present moment, focused on what you can see, hear and feel, for at least one minute (maybe set a timer).
- Thoughts will come into your mind (that is how minds work). Note the thought, gently.
- Gently let it go, and come back to noticing what is in the present.
- You might find that your mind has taken you off on a long diversion – planned the next day's agenda, gone over some incident that happened earlier, for instance.
- Gently note where your mind has taken you, and just as gently lead it back to noticing, for instance, what it feels like to breathe, in the present.
- Let go of any judgements about slipping in your intention to be mindful of the present; the fact that you noticed what your mind was doing and brought it back means that you were being truly mindful.

You can congratulate yourself. After all, minds have a mind of their own – and there is no boss!

Once you have got the hang of doing this exercise for a minute, extend the time that you spend noticing thoughts, slowly.

Behaviour changing strategy ♘

Worksheet 7C: Mindfulness practice

Use the following chart to log your regular mindfulness practice. If you are not sure why you are doing this – trust me, all will become clear! When you manage a brief mindfulness session, note down for how long and what you noticed.

Day	Morning	Afternoon	Evening
Monday			
Tuesday			
Wednesday			
Thursday			
Friday			
Saturday			
Sunday			

Keeping up with regular mindfulness practice and logging it will be extremely helpful when it comes to noticing your thinking style and doing something about it. We have already seen how powerful thinking styles are in keeping people stuck with their anger. Now is the point to start doing something about that!

Clearly, noticing what you are thinking lies at the heart of this. In the next chapters, we will consider substituting different, more helpful and less 'stuck' ways of thinking. Before you can do that, you need to become good at noticing what you are thinking and being able to stand back from it. This is where thought monitoring comes in – and here is the worksheet for this!

Reviewing behaviour

Worksheet 7D: Noticing thoughts

This worksheet invites you to:

- look at situations that have got to you; remember, anything that gets to you is important – it does not need to be full-blown anger
- identify what immediate coping technique you used, e.g. breathing, mindfulness
- identify your thoughts.

Date and time	What was happening	Immediate coping	What thoughts went through your mind?

Chapter summary

In this chapter we have seen what a powerful role thoughts can play in sparking anger and keeping it going. We have explained how this is tied to the theory of cognitive behavioural therapy. You have also:

- learned about the different types of wind-up thinking, with examples of how such thinking can take over people's lives with bad consequences
- been introduced to mindfulness of thoughts
- been encouraged to undertake regular mindfulness practice
- been encouraged to start monitoring your thoughts whenever you feel angry or something 'gets to you'.

You should now be in a good position to go forward to find more helpful ways of thinking in Chapter 8, and so loosen the grip that anger may have had on your life.

Alternatives to wind-up thinking

Overview

In Chapter 7 you learned how the way you are thinking helps to make you angry and keep you angry. This led onto work on starting to identify your thoughts. Now it is time to look for alternative thoughts; thoughts that will not keep you angry. This chapter covers:

- recognizing that thoughts are not facts
- acknowledging how hard it can be to let go of thoughts
- revenge as an example of thoughts that people find it hard to step away from
- working out for yourself the pros and cons of adopting less wind-up ways of thinking
- good reasons for letting go of thoughts and developing the mental flexibility to find alternative thoughts
- case studies illustrating the struggle to find alternative ways of thinking.
- how to counter the typical unhelpful ways of thinking identified in Chapter 7.

Monitoring your progress

How did you get on with mindfulness of thoughts? If you gave that a go, I would be surprised if you did not notice your mind wandering into the past or the future. That is because the past and the future is where minds are most comfortable. Staying in the present is like trying to stay balanced on a very narrow, uncomfortable bar. You're always wanting to slip off to one side or the other. But remember, to have any hope of control over your life, the present is the place you have got to be at the moment when you take control – being aware all the time that you can never have that much control, because there is no boss!

Did you manage to increase the number of minutes you spent in mindfulness practice (Worksheet 7C)? Keep on letting those minutes creep up. See if you can get to five or ten minutes.

How did you get on with noticing thoughts (Worksheet 7D)? Even if you had a 'good' week and nothing much happened that was annoying, I hope you noticed some times when your calm was disturbed and managed to catch the thoughts behind those moments. This is such important information – it will really help you to understand your anger and to change your reaction to it.

Did you notice some of the wind-up thinking categories listed in Chapter 7? What are your most commonly used ones? Have you started to notice other peoples' wind-up thinking? Listen carefully to the words they use and spot the telltale 'should', 'must', 'it's not fair' statements etc. The more aware of that you can become, the better you are doing.

Finding a different way of thinking

Behind the practice of becoming aware of wind-up thinking is the idea that you have a choice about how you think about things. If it is something you do not feel strongly about, that is not difficult. For example, someone might think: 'I would never want to have a black car'. But when they need to change their car at short notice and a trusted friend offers them a great deal on a black car … they change their mind: black cars are really rather smart.

That is a simple example of finding a different way of thinking: circumstances change. The old way of thinking is no longer convenient. Find a new one! Can you think of examples of when you have changed your mind, found a different way of thinking, like that?

Sometimes changing your thinking is harder. Circumstances mean that you have to let go of a way of thinking that you are really attached to. Sometimes it feels impossible. In those cases, it does not feel like a way of thinking. It feels like a fact. Take the example of Gary from one of the groups.

Case study: Gary (1)

Gary's problems started when the factory where he had worked for 20 years since leaving school closed down. His life had settled into a rigid pattern which was now shattered. His attempts to get another job came to nothing – those sort of jobs did not exist any more. His wife was now the breadwinner on top of her other roles of running the household and taking responsibility for the three children. As Gary was now at home all day, she not unreasonably tried to involve him in taking his share. He felt both out of his depth and inadequate that he did not have a job, but instead of saying so (probably because he did not even realize it), he reacted with indignation at being asked to do 'women's work'. After all, a woman should do the housework. The man should go out and earn the money.

As far as Gary was concerned, his ideas about the roles of men and women were not 'his thoughts'; they were a description of how things should be – they were facts.

So when Gary got to the 'finding a different way of thinking' session of the anger management course, did he manage to find that flexibility?

Thoughts and facts

It is when we are in the Emotion Mind that thoughts feel most like facts. A branch of CBT called acceptance and commitment therapy (ACT) refers to this as 'fusion' because the thought becomes stuck or fused (Hayes et al., 1999). In order to loosen the grip of wind-up thinking, it is necessary to realize that thoughts are not facts; that things can be thought about in different ways; and that this flexibility of thinking is necessary in order to get a grip on anger.

It is useful when working on thinking styles to recognize the role of the Emotion Mind in reducing flexibility – that is why using breathing and mindfulness to switch out of 'action mode' is the foundation of any anger management. It is easy to forget those techniques as more ideas get added and things get more complicated. Whenever you find yourself slipping, when it starts to get hard not to lose your temper, remember to go back to the body, the breathing, and attend to that foundation.

Case study: Gary (2)

When Gary did the homework, logging his thinking about his situation, he realized it was full of 'shoulds': women *should* be the ones to do the housework, and the central problem that someone *should* be giving him a job so that he could hold his head high and lead the life that a man ought to. Accepting that the situation had changed was hard for Gary. It meant accepting that hanging onto those *shoulds* was getting him nowhere. It could lose him his wife, family and home on top of his job if he did not make some changes. It was the other members of the group who helped him to see that not everyone thought like that. Some of the other men explained that they were prepared to help out in the house; they could see where Gary was coming from, but the world had changed. They helped him to come up with an alternative way of thinking. 'As I am at home, maybe I should take my turn. She needs a bit of a hand and it will help to keep the peace.'

Letting go is hard

It is always possible to find different ways to think about things, but that does not mean that it is easy. Letting go of his 'shoulds' was not easy for Gary. That way of thinking 'felt' right and letting go of it felt like a sort of defeat – a giving-in to a reality that he did not want to accept. It was only when he realized how much was at stake, how much he stood to lose if he clung onto it, that he was prepared to consider it. Then the others in the group, whom he had come to trust and to identify with, helped him to find a different way of looking at things.

There are always going to be good reasons for hanging onto wind-up thinking, based fundamentally on what it 'feels' like. It sometimes feel quite dangerous to let go of this thinking; it means stepping out into a scary unknown – in Gary's case, a world where the roles of men and women are turned upside down. Then again, it can feel like defeat; letting *them* (whoever *they* are) get away with it. That can be really difficult. Thoughts to do with revenge are often particularly hard to let go of.

Revenge and the group

The anger management group was always run by a team of two or three health professionals – nurses, doctors, occupational therapists, psychologists etc. – who were either in training or wanting more training in CBT. Close supervision by me was an important part both of this learning process and of keeping the group on track, and as we have already seen, anger management groups could be quite hard work to keep on track. The facilitators had to remain on top of the agenda, but one topic that regularly threatened to derail this was the subject of revenge. Revenge usually cropped at some point in a group, and tended to unite the participants in opposition to the facilitators. The facilitators considered that plotting revenge was a bad thing. The group invariably seized on the idea with enthusiasm. Plotting revenge is a good example of 'you or the world' wind-up thinking. The idea that *they* are not going to get away with it and *you* will get your own back can feel very attractive, and things that are attractive, that make one feel good, are really hard to let go of.

In the supervision that followed a group like this, I would coach the dispirited facilitators to remind the group members why they had joined the course; get them to take a step back and remember why changing their relationship with anger was important for them. By the time we were looking at thoughts and revenge came up, they had been working on getting control over their bodies' action mode and noticing how much calmer they had become; how much easier it was not to overreact. Then we got them to notice what effect plotting revenge had on the body and to notice how it was necessary to keep thinking wind-up thoughts in order to maintain the momentum of plotting revenge. From there it was possible to get them to recognize that plotting revenge meant they were undoing all the good work that had been achieved. If they hung onto wind-up revenge thoughts, all their other anger thoughts would also stay in place. Did they really want to throw away everything they had achieved over several weeks and go back to square one? That generally did the trick!

Reviewing behaviour

Worksheet 8A

What are your most commonly used types of wind-up thinking? Have a look at your Worksheet 7D, and write down any more that occur to you after reading this chapter.

- How do you feel about letting go of these thoughts?
- What makes it difficult to let go of them?

Sometimes it is helpful to take these reservations seriously, as well as looking at the reasons for change, by filling in a worksheet like this one and identifying for each thought:

- the disadvantages of letting it go (i.e. reasons for keeping it)
- the advantages of letting it go (i.e. reasons for not keeping it).

Thought	Disadvantages of letting go	Advantages of letting go

Finding an alternative thought

I have said a lot about the way your body can tell you what to do, often in ways that are not in your best interests, like getting into fights. Now is the time to turn the tables. How about getting your body to help you to do what you choose? This works because of the very immediate connection between the body and the mind that manages to bypass the slow, cumbersome thinking bit of the brain. Consider when you are feeling unconfident and a bit awkward. The natural way to hold yourself is with your head down, trying to make yourself small. Then you decide you want to take control of the situation. You decide to hold your head high and your body straight. Stride forward. Even if this starts off feeling like acting, it usually works – you actually do feel more confident.

Now let's apply that to letting go of a stubborn wind-up thought, to make space for a different way of thinking. Simply shrug it off. Literally! Give your shoulders a shrug, relax your whole body as the shrug goes downward, letting the tension run off with it. Feel the thought dislodging itself and getting shrugged off along with the tension. Then hold your head high. Say to yourself 'I am in charge now', and try out the new way of thinking for size.

Once you have got your body on-side and let go of the tension keeping your thinking rigid, you can start to look around for other ways of thinking. This is all about mental flexibility and, as with physical flexibility, practice is key. You have probably had a lot of practice thinking about things in particular ways. Most people have by the time they reach adulthood. You now need to make an effort to look at the same things differently: to get different viewpoints, different perspectives.

Reasons for replacing wind-up thinking

Wind-up thinking and the past

Remember the Emotion Mind and Reasonable Mind (Chapter 2)? The Emotion Mind has its own memory. This memory stores anything that has been threatening for you throughout your life – just in case, to keep you safe. These memories are triggered again by things happening in the present that have some echo of that past threat. This means that the more you allow wind-up thinking free rein, the more that past threat stays alive for you. For many people, the past is much better left in the past; that certainly goes for most of the people in the case studies in this book. It is bad enough having to deal with all the trouble that happens in the present without having your rotten childhood or bullies at school, or whatever, pursuing you through your life! The key to freeing yourself from the past is to address that wind-up thinking and substitute an alternative.

Keeping your self-respect

Other people's anger can be hilarious. Remember Mick in Chapter 4? When he was able to stand back from the situation using the breathing exercise, he was able to notice that his mates were winding him up for the fun of watching him lose his rag. Think of your favourite comedy show or film. Were there some good scenes of someone being angry? Can you remember what made it so funny? Think about seeing someone else lose their temper. How did they come across to others? Is that how you want others to see you? Even if you are not fully convinced by your alternative to wind-up thinking, it is worth trying to go with it just to keep your dignity and self-respect. This does not mean that you will become a pushover. Far from it. We will look at how to get your point across in less confrontational ways in Chapter 11.

Phrases to help you shift perspective

- 'Let it go.'
- 'So what?'
- 'In the grand scheme of things, compared with …' [think of a war or disaster featured on the news at the moment/the defeat of your favourite football club by San Marino etc. – you get the idea!]

- 'Life is too short …'
- 'It's not a bad world. Just badly organized.'

Can you come up with some good ones for yourself? List at least three.

_____

_____

_____

_____

_____

Here is an example where letting go of the wind-up thinking was really difficult. The key to letting go was recognizing how the wind-up thinking was keeping the anger alive and that it was keeping in the present a past that needed to be put in the past.

Case study: Jock (1)

Jock's Scottish background was a hard one. He came south to give himself a better chance, and things worked quite well for a couple of decades. He was good at his trade, earned good money, got married and had a couple of children. However, he always hung onto his quick temper as he always had the sense that someone was trying to do him down, and he had never liked himself. He drank quite a lot – partly habit, and partly because that let him escape himself.

Then things went seriously wrong. He got into a fight at work and someone was badly hurt; he was charged and spent a short spell in prison. He lost his job and his marriage through that, and when he got out of prison, he hit the bottle really badly and found himself on the streets. At this point he was extremely angry with the world for giving him a raw deal: he felt the sentence was very unfair as the man he had hurt had provoked him; he thought his wife should have stuck by him, and losing the kids felt really painful. Drink helped to numb that pain.

Things turned around. A worker at a hostel where he dossed helped him to stay sober long enough to get a job and, importantly, helped him track his children through social media. His son was trying to find him. That gave Jock the push he needed to tackle his temper, but the burning resentment against the people he felt had lost him those years of his life remained, and as a result his anger was always near the surface and difficult to control, even though he worked hard all the way through the course. When he got to the session on wind-up thinking, this came out into the open. Some unfairness at work would immediately get him thinking about the unfairness of his sentence. He just could not come up with an alternative because of the way he was thinking: 'I can't let it go because then they would win'. The group and the facilitators agreed that what had happened to him in the past probably was very unfair, but they really wanted Jock to be able to move on in his life. They managed to get him to see that hanging onto those wind-up thoughts was actually keeping the past alive, and so in a sense 'they' were winning. 'Let it go, then I win' was worked out as an acceptable alternative thought that helped Jock to live in his more hopeful present and future.

Alternatives to unhelpful ways of thinking

I hope you can now see the point of working on letting go of your common wind-up thoughts and substituting different ways of thinking that will enable you to approach the future more calmly. Here are some tips on how to find alternatives to the different categories of wind-up thinking identified in Chapter 7.

Unhelpful ways of thinking	Examples of unhelpful ways of thinking	Examples of alternative ways of thinking
Should, must and ought	People who drive like that *ought not* to be allowed on the road.	It is regrettable that not every driver is as competent as I am, but at least I have the skills to avoid the worst.
	People *should* agree with my point of view.	It would be nice to live in a world where everyone agreed with me – but unrealistic and possibly a bit boring.

(Continued)

Unhelpful ways of thinking	Examples of unhelpful ways of thinking	Examples of alternative ways of thinking
		Everyone is entitled to their own opinion. I am entitled to mine.
All-or-nothing thinking	I can't get this wallpaper to hang perfectly. I'm going to give up.	I will simply have to learn to tolerate my annoyance when I notice the fault in the paper-hanging. With a bit of luck, if I don't say anything about it, no one else will remark on it – and even if they do, I will explain that I tried my best and that will have to do.
	This course hasn't stopped me from losing my temper yet. It's obviously useless. I'm going to leave.	Give the course time. Maybe I need to carry on practising before I see results. After all, it has helped other people with quite bad problems.
Over-generalization	So the meal isn't ready yet. You are *always* late.	This is annoying. I am hungry and I want to go out afterwards, but it will be good when it comes.
	You can *never* organize anything.	OK, she/he is not as organized as I am, but does have other qualities, and I am glad we are together.

Jumping to conclusions	She didn't say 'hello'; she's deliberately ignoring me.	She probably didn't see me.
	The boss was in a hurry to get away when I tackled him about my career. He obviously doesn't value me – he probably wants to get rid of me.	A shame I didn't manage to have that important conversation as a lot hangs on it – but better to have it at a time when she/he can really give me their attention.
You or the world	It must be my fault that those two members have stopped coming to the group. I always thought they didn't like me.	There are plenty of reasons why someone might stop coming – I have thought about it myself, after all!
	I couldn't help being late – there's nothing I can do about it if the motorway is clogged up with idiots and the council chooses now to dig up the road.	OK, maybe I was a bit unrealistic in my estimate of how long it would take, and those roadworks have been there a while, so maybe I could have allowed a bit longer.

Behaviour changing strategy

Worksheet 8B

Carry on with the mindfulness practice, as in Worksheet 7C. It will help you to notice the thoughts before they take over, and to experience thoughts as thoughts, not facts. (Remember about fusion!)

Day	Morning	Afternoon	Evening
Monday			
Tuesday			
Wednesday			
Thursday			
Friday			
Saturday			
Sunday			

Now you need to continue to notice the wind-up thoughts; remember these can come to you even if there is no major upset – extra physical tension gives you the clue that they are hovering around! And then you need to log an alternative thought.

In CBT, it is usual to look at this alternative thought and ask yourself: How much do I believe this thought? If 10 was 100 per cent belief, and 0 was 'don't believe it at all', what number should I give it? Rating the strength of your belief is useful because when you start to come up with alternative thoughts, it might just be an exercise. If you don't believe the new thought at all, it is not going to help you to be less wound-up, but give it time. You can work on getting your mind around different ways of thinking, and by and by you might find yourself shifting – first towards half believing it, and then to giving it enough space that the old thought does not grip you nearly as much. No need to believe 100 per cent. The sort of flexible thinking we are aiming at is happy with a degree of doubt!

Behaviour changing strategy

Worksheet 8C: Alternative thinking

This worksheet invites you to:

- look at situations that have got to you
- identify your unhelpful thoughts
- come up with an alternative thought
- rate the strength of your belief in the alternative thought from 1 to 10, where 10 = believe completely and 1 = don't believe at all.

Date and time	What was happening?	What thoughts went through your mind?	Alternative thought	Belief rating (1–10)

Date and time	What was happening?	What thoughts went through your mind?	Alternative thought	Belief rating (1–10)

Chapter summary

After reading this chapter, you have learned:

- to recognize that thoughts are not facts
- how hard it can be to let go of certain ways of thinking
- to work out the advantages and disadvantages of adopting less wind-up ways of thinking
- reasons for letting go of thoughts and developing the mental flexibility to find alternative thoughts
- some ways to counter the typical unhelpful ways of thinking identified in Chapter 7.
- from the examples of how people were helped to find alternative ways of thinking when that was very difficult for them.

CHAPTER 9

Letting go of chronic stress

Overview

In this chapter we return to the body in order to:

- understand chronic stress
- understand the physical effects of chronic stress
- understand how chronic stress makes anger problems worse
- examine the barriers to letting go of chronic stress
- consider lifestyle changes to help let go of chronic stress

Monitoring your progress

Although we are switching to another topic, it does not mean we can forget about monitoring thoughts and coming up with alternatives. How is that going? Even if the topics are going to range more widely from now on, it is a good idea to keep up with the worksheets about thinking until noticing and revising your thinking patterns become second nature – believe me, you will get very good at it if you work at it.

Keep up the regular mindfulness too!

Chronic stress: what it is and where it comes from

We have just spent a couple of chapters considering the impact of thoughts and thinking styles on anger. These chapters followed chapters where the spotlight was on the body and the crucial role that the body plays in the anger response. It is time to turn attention back to the body, looking at how a habit of wind-up thinking goes hand in hand with chronic stress, and how they work together to strengthen each other. The consequence of this is that it can be really hard to escape from their double grip and let go of being an angry and bitter person. However, a brief look at chronic stress and its terrible effect on health and wellbeing should convince you that getting free of this double grip is absolutely essential.

In Chapter 4 we looked at how the body switches into 'action mode' when it gets the idea that it faces a threat, and how it can easily get the wrong end of the stick in its conclusions about threat. Even if there is something the matter that needs attention, fighting or running away are rarely helpful responses, but they are the only reactions that your body has to offer. We then saw how our minds take the cue from the body and its action response and start to look out for threat – which guarantees seeing threats all over the place! Then, because at this point the Emotion Mind circuits in our brains have taken over, a sense of time is lost and the feeling of being under threat that is driving this could relate to something very real but that happened a long time ago. As if that was not enough, we have seen in the last few chapters how brooding on wind-up thinking can keep the sense of threat alive long after the initial trigger has died down, whether through plotting revenge, mulling over the unfairness of the situation or vowing that 'they' should not win or 'get away with it'.

So how does all this affect us as human beings? It is starting to look as if 'action mode' could become permanent if we are not careful. This is not good news. Action mode, or (to use the technical term) the sympathetic nervous system, is only designed for emergencies. We are supposed to conduct our day-to-day life in the other mode, with the parasympathetic nervous system in charge. The table below clarifies the different modes of operating of each of these two systems.

Part of body	Parasympathetic nervous system	Sympathetic nervous system
Nervous system	Normal state for the body. It is the state that the body returns to after an episode in which adrenaline triggered the sympathetic nervous system has ended and the adrenalin has left the body	Triggered by sense of threat followed by release of adrenaline
Heart rate	Normal rate and rhythm No extra exertion needed You don't notice it	Heart rate speeds up For vigorous action you need extra blood in all your limbs and organs; the heart achieves this by pumping blood round faster
Breathing	You breathe evenly You are likely to be unaware of the fact that you are breathing	You breathe in fast, and breathe out less When you engage in vigorous action, you need plenty of oxygen and use it up quickly, hence gulping it in rapid, short breaths. If you are not physically active, this type of breathing upsets the balance of oxygen and carbon dioxide in the brain and can lead to panic, confusion and loss of control (temper)
Muscles	These follow the normal rhythm of relaxation and tension to enable you to hold your body	You feel tense, sometimes leading to shaking and tremor in the limbs, and pain if prolonged

(Continued)

Part of body	Parasympathetic nervous system	Sympathetic nervous system
	comfortably and use your limbs efficiently, without you having to think about it	Tension in the head and face muscles can lead to headache
		Muscles become tense because extra blood and oxygen are being sent to the muscles so that your legs can run away fast or your arms fight effectively
Stomach and digestive system	This gets on with the business of digesting your food and sorting it for absorption or excretion	You notice sensations such 'butterflies' or other uncomfortable feelings in the stomach, feeling sick or needing the toilet
	Unless you have eaten something problematic, you are unaware of the system working	Digestion etc. is switched off when there is an emergency so that resources (blood) can be withdrawn from the less essential parts of the system and redistributed to those that are vital for fight or flight
	You respond normally to hunger and need to use the toilet	
Thinking	You can choose where to focus your thoughts – you can home in on detail or take in the bigger picture	Your thinking becomes focused on threat (tunnel vision), fails to take in the bigger picture and, if prolonged, leads to confusion
	You are in charge	You have the sense that threat has taken over and is directing what you think

We need both the parasympathetic and the sympathetic nervous systems in order to be able to respond rapidly and appropriately to real emergencies. I am eternally grateful that my husband's threat system was alerted by noting a heavy chunk of concrete detaching itself from the ceiling of our rented apartment 43 years ago – grateful because it was about to fall on the playpen with our six-month-old son in it. Action mode enabled him to leap up and grab the playpen out of the way just in time – it may be 43 years ago, but feels like yesterday! That is an example of the sympathetic nervous system springing into action appropriately and saving life. Once the emergency is past, the parasympathetic system takes over and normal life resumes.

The problem is that moving backwards and forwards between the two systems does not always happen. For many of the reasons summarized above, it is very easy to get stuck in action mode, with the sympathetic system in charge all the time. This is known as chronic stress. In our society it is an extremely common problem. A recent estimate suggested that 39 per cent of work-related illnesses were caused by either stress, anxiety or depression – and anxiety and depression are not a million miles from stress! The image described in the box below is intended to get across the reality that chronic stress is not good for the system as a whole.

Second gear on the motorway

Consider the sympathetic and parasympathetic nervous systems as being like the gears in a car – except that there are only two of them. The parasympathetic system is fourth or fifth gear, for comfortable cruising or bombing steadily along the motorway. The sympathetic system is like second gear – what you need to get round a tight corner or on the approach to a busy roundabout.

Then imagine driving your car along the motorway at a steady 70 m.p.h. *in second gear!* Feels uncomfortable, doesn't it! Noisy. Inefficient. And worse, what is it doing to the engine? The gear box? Imagine the oil consumption? Doesn't bear thinking about, does it? That is what you are doing to your body if you are running it in action mode all the time, on the look-out for threat and with the sympathetic nervous system in charge. (Sympathetic is a really unhelpful name in the circumstances!)

Chronic stress and physical health

The second gear image emphasizes that chronic stress is a damaging way to run a human body. We will look at this in more detail by going through how the different parts of the body are affected when a healthy balance between the sympathetic and parasympathetic systems is disrupted by the sympathetic system remaining permanently on the alert.

The heart

People who react more to stress have a higher risk of cardiovascular disease. This risk is particularly linked to people who tend to be excessively competitive, impatient and hostile and who move and talk quickly. Interestingly, hostility has been identified as the most significant of these characteristics.

Another vicious circle that can further endanger the health of the heart is comfort eating in response to stress – reaching for easily available foods that are high in salt, sugar and fat.

Blood pressure

This is linked to the heart pumping faster as a stress response. The risks associated with high blood pressure and the resulting hypertension are serious: stroke, heart failure, kidney failure and heart attack.

The immune system

The immune system protects the body from infection, but stress undermines the immune system. This makes you more likely to succumb to any infection that is doing the rounds. However, there are also serious autoimmune conditions that may be triggered or made worse by stress; autoimmune diseases include arthritis and multiple sclerosis.

Pain

Continually tensing the muscles through prolonged stress can lead to muscular pain, such as backache, or to other consequences, such as grinding one's teeth. Back, shoulder and neck ache are extremely widespread. Any pain is both intensified and prolonged by stress. Migraine and headaches are a common example of pain in which stress plays a crucial role.

Diabetes

There is some evidence that chronic stress may lead to insulin-dependent diabetes in people who are predisposed to the disease. It could be that stress causes the immune system to destroy insulin-producing cells.

Other problems

Skin problems, such as acne, psoriasis and eczema, and the digestive disorder known as irritable bowel system are also related to stress. Stress could be implicated in tinnitus. It has also been linked to infertility. I doubt that this list is comprehensive.

The link between chronic stress, anger and physical health problems is illustrated by the case of Ahmed.

Case study: Ahmed (1)

Ahmed's wife, the most gentle and supportive person imaginable, happened to remark that her husband always seemed to be angry, and that this had not always been so. This got him thinking. Now in his fifties, he had a successful career in information technology, a nice house in a good part of town and three wonderful children. However, he could see that stress had built steadily over the past 10 years or so. It probably started when his local government department was outsourced to a private company. The pressure at work stepped up. People were made redundant. Youngsters were promoted over him, and questions were asked about his speed and competence at his job. He didn't want to think about it, but it looked as though he was being eased out. He responded by working all the hours he could as hard as he could; he dreaded the idea of losing his job and his status in the community and refused to face the possibility.

Then there were his children, now teenagers. His son could not be faulted, and his eldest daughter was devout to a fault – but the way in

---

which she had confronted the school governors to establish the right to wear the burka at school, although he could not help admiring her, also disturbed him. His beautiful 16-year-old younger daughter, the apple of his eye, was the most worrying. She was not allowed to go out in the evenings, but where was she between school and teatime? Snatches of conversation between his wife and her relatives suggested something worrying. It all got him feeling very suspicious. Sensing threat on every side but not able to confront it, Ahmed's stress levels, and with it his irritability, continued to grow.

A visit to the GP was the wake-up call. A collapse during Ramadan led to the diagnosis of diabetes, along with serious hypertension and heart irregularity. The GP was forthright: Ahmed needed to slow down and stop storing up worry if he was going to survive.

I wonder whether any of this feels familiar to you?

Stress symptoms list

Worksheet 9A

Make a note of any symptoms of chronic stress you may have noticed.

_____

_____

_____

Are you experiencing any physical health problems that could be linked to it?

_____

_____

_____

Now, thinking of the case of Ahmed, list the pressures that you find yourself under that might be leading to that stress.

_____

_____

_____

> Are there too many demands coming from too many sides? Are there
> worries that it is hard to face up to and deal with?
>
> _____
>
> _____
>
> _____

So, chronic stress is a real health risk, and feeling constantly under threat and therefore angry is how it builds up and is kept going.

The major part that chronic stress plays in anger problems makes it particularly relevant to this book. It is usually the culprit underlying the 'I am perfectly all right and then suddenly go ballistic over something minor' situation – that was Mick in Chapter 2, and something I've heard from many of the people I assessed for the anger management programme. Often what really bothered them was how trivial the actual cause of their anger had been – something they could see afterwards on reflection. At the time it felt important enough to merit a blazing row. One woman recalled her shame at having hurled a heavy ashtray at her boyfriend because he had put it down 'in the wrong place'.

That sort of reaction does not come from nowhere. It is the result of a build-up – a build-up of stress to the point where the next thing that comes along, however trivial, will tip the person over into full-blown rage. The best way to understand this is to look at Figure 9.1.

Everyone, no matter how laid-back and peaceable, has a point at which they will react to a stressful event with either loss of temper or panic (or both). It is a physiological fact that there is a limit beyond which the Reasonable Mind (remember Figure 2.1) can no longer function and the Emotion Mind or sheer confusion takes over. What Figure 9.1 illustrates is that when your normal level of stress is low, it takes something massive to tip you over that line. When your normal level of stress is very high, as in chronic stress, you are constantly near to that line and so anything can push you over the limit – hence a lot of really irrational reactions.

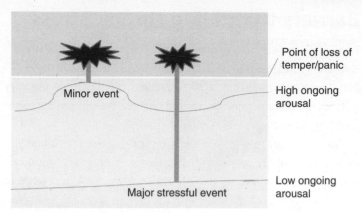

Figure 9.1: Effect of level of arousal on loss of temper/panic

Stress triggers list ✏️

Worksheet 9B

Can you recall some examples of times when you got very angry about something that you later realized was really unimportant? This sort of thing can happen to anyone when they are stressed, under pressure, overtired etc. – remember the disinhibitors in Chapter 3.

_____

_____

_____

_____

You might have noticed this with other people? When someone reacts irrationally like this, it makes great comedy. Can you think of examples from a favourite comedy series or film? Write down as many examples as you can think of.

_____

_____

_____

_____

Barriers to tackling chronic stress

I hope this chapter has got across the point that chronic stress is something that needs to be dealt with – urgently and effectively. However, as with so much to do with anger, tackling it can feel very difficult, even dangerous, despite the fact that the real danger comes from the stress.

The reason for this is the underlying sense of threat that many people, particularly people with an anger problem, carry around deep inside themselves. As we have seen earlier in the book, this sense of threat probably has little to do with the present situation, and is more to do with terrifying events the person suffered earlier in life. No matter that these are in the past, the Emotion Mind keeps the sense of threat in the forefront of the mind. And the more stressed you are, the more the Emotion Mind is in control and the past overtakes the present! For this reason, people often feel that they need to be constantly on the alert for danger, keeping their sympathetic nervous system at the ready, and leading to chronic stress. Josh provides a good example both of how this can happen and of how a group session helped him to recognize that he had to address it, however much it 'felt' like the wrong thing to do!

Case study Josh (3)

Five years after he initially left the group in anger, Josh returned to the programme. A lot had happened in those five years. Unsurprisingly, Carmen had left after a serious assault. Then came a prison term. In many ways this was a turning point. Because Josh blamed his mates in the drug trade for the conviction – they had failed to shield him sufficiently, and may have pointed the law in his direction to save themselves – this motivated him to cut himself off from them, to avoid drugs in prison and to take advantage of education and skill-learning opportunities. Also, his quiet but firm new girlfriend, Asha, would not tolerate drugs and he felt very responsible for her. Her (Asian) family had rejected her because of him, as he was black Caribbean.

A sticking point came in session nine. Josh felt constantly under threat and was convinced that he needed to remain at a high level of readiness to go on the attack if he was to defend both himself and Asha. To let go of that would be to let the hostile forces take over. Josh came to session 10 with a homework example that really bothered him. He had shouted aggressively at Asha and terrified her. He could see now that the trigger for this anger was trivial. The facilitator gently pointed out the way that keeping stress levels constantly high made managing his anger ten times harder. However unsafe it felt, the only way to stop such things happening again was to work at lowering his constant readiness to go on the attack. Josh finally realized that this was the only way to be truly safe. As a bonus, this would help him to let go of his violent and dangerous past and work on establishing a new present.

Lifestyle changes to manage chronic stress

So, how do you do let go of chronic stress?

Exercise

As stress is about your body being constantly ready for action, but without getting any, regular exercise is a good stress-buster. Look at what exercise you do now. Is there scope for an increase? A good place to start is to come up with a regular journey that can be done on foot or by bicycle in preference to using the car. If you decide to join a gym, walk there.

Swimming is very good exercise, and usually possible for people who have physical problems that restrict other forms of exercise. Recreations such as country walks and gardening provide exercise (with gardening this is quite varied, involving lifting etc.) as well as an opportunity to live in the moment in natural surroundings – good mindfulness practice!

A word of warning, however; exercise undertaken in a competitive, including a self-competitive, spirit can increase arousal levels and so can have the opposite effect to what you want. If you enter your exercise in a 'fighting' spirit, it is hardly surprising if that switches on the 'fight or flight' response! More on that in Chapter 10.

Tackle stressors and worries

Stress comes from having demands placed on you, or placing demands on yourself, that you cannot meet. To escape from chronic stress you need to do some hard-headed sifting of the demands on you and find a way to reduce them if they are too great. This may mean facing up to things like negotiating with people – certainly talking to people.

Go through the sort of exercise suggested for instances of anger, but this time for stress and worry, making lists of the things that are on your mind because you have got to do them (Worksheet 9C) and the things you are worrying about (Worksheet 9D).

Beware of perfectionism and of trying to please everybody. Use mindfulness (see below) to manage the uncomfortable feeling you get when things are not completed to your satisfaction, or you have to set limits with someone.

Use assertiveness where necessary to explain to others the limits of what you can manage (see Chapter 11).

Allow for a balance between duty and pleasurable activities – find more things that give you satisfaction and that you enjoy to include in your life.

Behaviour changing strategy

Worksheet 9C: Tackling stressors

Write down all the things you need to do, and then break each of the things down into:

- things you can get on with
- things you are not sure how to tackle
- things over which you have no control and need to let go of.

Consider the things you are not sure how to tackle: how can you make these more manageable, and what can you let go of?

- Use Worksheet 6B to help you problem-solve, prioritize and develop an action plan for doing the things you can tackle.
- If there are too many things to tackle, concentrate on the priority ones and add the others to the last column of things that are too much and that you need to let go of.

Things I need to do	Of these:		
	Things I can get on with	Things I am not sure how to tackle	Things that are too much

Now go through the same process with your worries. Talking to someone is also a good idea when it comes to worries; it helps you to face things that you might have been trying to avoid.

Use your mindfulness (see below) to help you accept and let go of the worries you cannot do anything about.

Behaviour changing strategy

Worksheet 9D: Tackling worries

Write down the things you are worrying about, and then separate the worries into:

- things you can deal with, even if you are not sure how at first
- things over which you have no control and need to accept and let go.

Consider the things you can deal with but are not sure how to tackle. Use Worksheet 6B to help you problem-solve and prioritize these and develop an action plan.

My worries	Worries I can deal with (e.g. by problem-solving)	Worries I need to accept and let go

Use mindfulness

Chapter 5 explained how mindfulness was first introduced into therapy as a stress reduction tool, and it remains a powerful and effective one. If you have been following this book faithfully, you will already be practising mindfulness regularly. If not, now is the time to go back and take the mindfulness sections seriously. The following exercise is designed to help you let go of worries.

Practical help ⇨

Mindfulness exercise: Letting go of worries

- Bring yourself into the present.
- Be aware of your body, your surroundings, your breathing.
- Be aware of your thoughts.
- Be aware that they are just thoughts.
- If the thoughts are emotional or stressful, note the effect they are having on your body.
- Notice where you experience this.
- Be aware that it is just your body reacting as it will – just an event in your body.
- Let go of both the thoughts and the tension in your body.
- Come back to being you in the present.
- You are more than both your thoughts and your body tension.

Be prepared to go through this again and again.

Increase enjoyable activities

Reducing stress is not just about making work and other obligations more manageable. It is, more importantly, about getting a better balance between those obligations and the satisfying, enjoyable things in life. Here is another problem-solving exercise; I will leave you to draw your own table for this one.

- What enjoyable activities would you like to add to your life?
- Can you problem-solve introducing one or two?

Another way of looking at this is to use mindfulness to get the maximum enjoyment out of fairly routine activities. This is particularly useful if you don't have much spare cash or the time to go on fabulous trips etc. During the walk to the local shops with a rucksack for your shopping that you are going to substitute for using the car, mindfully note what the clouds, the trees, the local dogs etc. are doing on your way. Gardening – which can feel like a chore – may shift if you approach it mindfully, noticing how you are present in nature, into pleasure. Spending time with or just observing animals, birds and other non-human creatures, whether your pets or animals and birds that are living wild, is another stress-reducing, mindful option.

Let's see how Ahmed tackled the challenge of reducing his chronic stress.

Case study: Ahmed (2)

Ahmed's GP took his situation seriously and insisted they have a talk about his lifestyle and what he could do to reduce stress.

Exercise

Ahmed was not keen on the idea of a prescription for the gym but managed to satisfy the doctor by promising to go on a daily walk round the local park, and to walk rather than drive to the mosque on Fridays.

Worries and stressors

The GP could see that these were the major part of the problem, but Ahmed kept asserting that nothing could be done about them. He did concede that he had not had a good talk to his wife about his worries concerning his daughters, and promised he would do this. He said he would think about the work situation. At this point, the GP let him go, along with a referral to the diabetic clinic.

Worries – the family

The talk with his wife was an eye-opener. The situation with his younger daughter's friendship with a boy his wife considered a concern, but a managed one. She had discussed it with her family, and as they knew the boy's family, it was agreed that the girl could spend time after school there, well-chaperoned, as they were considered to be sensible, steady young people and this is 21st-century Britain. The main worry about this situation had been Ahmed's reaction should he find out about the friendship. His wife was more concerned about the elder girl and the rather extreme faction from the mosque that she was involved with, but her real worry was their son. Who was he mixing with? Where had the money for the brand-new motorbike come from? Their son's story about a distant cousin had been checked and found to be false. She had not dared raise any of this with Ahmed for fear of his temper.

Clearly, none of this reduced the level of Ahmed's worries, but he did find that being confided in openly, being trusted and treated as the true head of the household, boosted his sense of self-worth. He realized how isolated he had been and how aware that a lot was going on that he knew nothing about. He could see how important it was that he talk to his children but without losing his temper. His wife was sure that both elder siblings would respect and listen to their father; such a talk would make all the difference, and Ahmed recognized that he had an important role here.

Stressors – the job

All this put his job into a different perspective. Ahmed felt as if scales had fallen from his eyes. His employer wanted rid of him and he needed to be rid of the job so that he could be present for the real job of being head of the household in his family. All it needed was to negotiate the best redundancy package he could manage – and he had a friend from the mosque with the skills to help there. He could suddenly see that he had perhaps been using the job to hide from the family without being aware of it.

Life satisfaction

The new role would be tough but would give him the satisfaction of being part of his family again – along with his prominent role in the local Muslim community. However, none of this was going to work without Ahmed mastering his anger so that the crucial conversations with his teenage children were conducted in a reasonable and reasoned spirit!

The monitoring to be done as 'homework' this week is to look at chronic stress and you. Using the worksheets and other exercises in this chapter, you are going to work out what changes are needed to your lifestyle to make life more manageable and satisfying, and then make a plan – your very own manageable life balance plan!

Behaviour changing strategy

Worksheet 9E: Your life balance plan

Using the worksheets and other exercises in this chapter, consider what changes you can make to your lifestyle that will make your life more manageable and satisfying.

- Exercise – what can be done here?
- Look at the balance between your work/obligations and the sources of enjoyment in your life – is any action needed? What can you improve here?
- Look at your stressors and worries tables – what actions do Worksheet 9C and 9D suggest?

You don't have to limit yourself to three items! Add as many as you think are manageable – when you've achieved those, you can always do this exercise again.

	Plan of action	When? How often?
Exercise 1		
2		
3		
Pleasurable activities 1		
2		
3		

	Plan of action to reduce/manage stress	When
Stressors 1		
2		
3		
Worries 1		
2		
3		

And don't forget to keep up your mindfulness practice. Use this both to manage worry and to increase your enjoyment and satisfaction in the simple things in life.

Chapter summary

In this chapter you have:

- learned what chronic stress is and its physical effects
- considered the role of chronic stress in your life
- looked at how chronic stress makes anger problems worse
- made a plan to manage stressors and worries in your life
- considered the barriers to letting go of chronic stress
- looked at what lifestyle changes help to let go of chronic stress
- constructed your own life balance plan.

CHAPTER 10

Obstacles and consolidation

Overview

This chapter first reviews where we have got to so far in the journey through this book. Then it looks at the factors that can complicate working on anger:

- physical injury, deterioration and disability
- head injury, brain injury and forms of dementia
- addiction and substance abuse
- mental health issues.

The chapter concludes by looking at how mindfulness can become a part of everyday life.

Monitoring your progress

How did you get on with reviewing your manageable life balance plan (Worksheet 9E)? Have you identified the stressors that keep you tense? Have you come up with lifestyle changes that will help? And, importantly, have you actually done anything new? Congratulate yourself if you have.

Look at your mindfulness monitoring. How are you doing keeping up with that?

Taking stock

Having reached Chapter 10, it is time to take stock. Anyone working their way through this book has already gone on quite a journey. They have been presented with a way of looking at anger, and indeed at human beings, that might be different from the one they were used to. Anger is seen as a potentially useful resource if managed well, and human beings are seen as much less 'together' than we like to think we are. We are constantly engaged in a balancing act between our emotional and reasonable minds, and trying to feel comfortable with ourselves and the world. We have seen how some people learn to use their out-of-control anger, and the fear this produces in those around them, to manage their lives, to manage the balancing act. It can almost become part of who they are. For this reason, giving it up is not easy. However, many people with this sort of relationship with anger find that it results in more losses than gains as life goes on, seeing relationships, children, jobs and even liberty slip away as a result of their temper.

Then we considered how to manage anger. Key to this was managing physical arousal; the 'fight or flight' response, or as I prefer to call it, the body getting ready for action. Mindfulness has become a major part of CBT since the time of the anger management programme on which much of this book is based, but as it is very useful as a way to manage the balance between the reasonable and emotion minds, mindfulness has been introduced here.

I hope that by now you are really good at using long, slow out-breaths to master 'action mode', and that your mindfulness practice is coming on nicely. The purpose of learning these skills is to be able to find that wobbly place where you are in touch both with your feelings and with your rational mind; what dialectical behaviour therapy calls the 'Wise Mind'. People often see the solution to anger problems in terms of switching off their emotions and switching into rational mode. We have argued that this is not a good strategy. The emotions don't go away; they are simply suppressed and build up under the surface to break out in a less manageable form in the future.

Also, anger itself has something important to tell you. This might be about things that need addressing here and now or it might be about the past, but that too is interesting. Further, it can supply the energy to tackle what is wrong once the rational part of the mind has problem-solved the best way forward. Choosing to manage your anger in this way rather than allowing the anger to take over can be challenging, but ultimately it is worthwhile in terms of self-respect and effectiveness.

We followed that by considering the role of thoughts in triggering and maintaining anger. Identifying and letting go of wind-up thinking is a central tool in anger management. Finally, we returned to the body and looked at the effects on it of chronic stress and how to do something about that.

From Chapter 11 onwards we pick up a major theme from Chapter 1: that of the relationship with oneself and with others, and the central importance of these relationships for human beings. In Part 3, we will look at anger in the context of relationships and explore different, sounder ways of managing those crucial relationships.

Obstacles to progress

Before moving on, we need to consider the obstacles that commonly get in the way of people trying to deal with their anger. These obstacles all essentially come down to the things that happen to people in their journey through life, how they respond to these events and experiences, and how this affects their anger and their ability to deal with it in the ways suggested by this book. None of the obstacles rules out the possibility of anger management. They just complicate it and call for more advanced problem-solving.

Physical injury, deterioration and disability

We tend to take our bodies for granted, but they are complex mechanisms that can go wrong or get damaged in a myriad ways. Some parts of the body are more prone to malfunction than others; backs are notoriously apt to give trouble; joints start to wear out with age. The longer we are alive, the greater the probability of sustaining an injury that we just have to learn to live with, and the greater the likelihood that we might start to lose our mental faculties. For some people, this will not affect their relationship with anger. For others, it does in a number of ways.

We have already seen how coping with unwelcome change can feel like a major threat, and injury leading to disability is just such a change. It can lead to a catalogue of losses in addition to physical function, such as the ability to do a job or earn as high a salary, and it can put a strain on relationships. All that is enough to spark an anger reaction in someone who tends to take things that way. 'It's not fair' is a completely understandable and natural reaction, difficult to answer, but a distinctly 'wind-up' response in those circumstances.

Even worse, physical injury can greatly limit the range of options for dealing with anger that are open to the individual. The case of Jed illustrates what was, unfortunately, a fairly common scenario in people I assessed for the anger management programme.

Case study: Jed

Jed had always been a driven individual, and his relations with others were never easy. However, his energy and drive had its plus side. He ran a small wholesale business on his own, a niche market that he had control of (which was how he liked it). He was on his second marriage and had young children, his older children being looked after by his ex-wife. All this kept him financially on his toes. However, he relished a high-stress, high-energy lifestyle, and his passion for running was his way of letting off steam (and his escape from domestic life, for which he had a low tolerance).

All this changed abruptly with a major back injury. Being laid up for a few months was aggravating, but even worse was the convalescence: learning to live with constant pain, having to take on a partner and delegate much of his business to him (Jed had deliberately avoided employing anyone before because he found it impossible to tolerate anyone deviating from his way of doing things) and, worst of all, having to give up running.

All this brought home to Jed that life would never be the same again. He was warned that he would always have to be cautious physically; he was advised to replace running with swimming, which he hated and the chlorine made him ill, and generally advised to slow down. Stuck at home with his wife and children, fuming at the way his new business partner was botching (in his view) the business, and with all his normal outlets closed, Jed's temper started to boil over with increasing frequency and force. His wife was frightened for herself and the children. His business partner threatened to leave.

Jed realized for the first time just how much his previous way of life had been propped up by working all hours at full drive and spending much of the rest of the time running off his pent-up frustrations. Without these outlets he had to face himself and his relationships with other people. A hard road of accepting the situation, rebuilding his relationship with himself and his family, and taking up the hated swimming lay ahead, or he stood to lose everything.

The example of Jed brings home just how crucial the outlet of physical activity can be in enabling some people to keep their anger in check, and what a difficult adjustment follows from no longer having that release.

Head injury, brain injury and forms of dementia

Physical injury and disability is hard enough to come to terms with, but what about when it affects the mind? What follows is a brief glance at a massive topic, where I have lumped together three different problems.

All three have in common with physical injury the challenge of facing up to a new and unwelcome situation in life and the sense of threat that goes with this. Head injury and brain injury often result from traumatic events such as accident, injury or (worse in terms of threat value) physical assault. However, brain injury can also be the result of illness, such as a tumour. In such cases, onset is more gradual; it creeps up on the sufferer. This less distinct start, harder to pinpoint but disquieting and disorienting in its own way, is generally characteristic of the various forms of dementia.

These conditions affect people differently, depending on which part of the brain is affected. The most common effects are on the memory, the ability to think and to plan, and on the emotions and personality. Obviously, if someone can no longer 'get their mind around' things in the way they used to, it makes life much more difficult, gets in the way of communication with other people and removes their confidence and ability to manage life. All these lead to frustration, a sense of unease and threat, and so anger. Difficulties in communication with other people are irritating and have the same result. Think of the problems that can occur in conversation with someone who is hard of hearing – misunderstandings and having to repeat things. The effects of brain injury, damage and dementia are often more far-reaching and so even more frustrating.

As if all this were not bad enough, the effects on emotions and personality are often more serious.

Frontal lobe brain damage

The frontal lobes of our brain are a vital part of the 'new brain', the part of our thinking apparatus that developed most recently in evolutionary terms. It is when a part of the brain is damaged that we really learn what its function is, and the frontal lobes have several very significant functions. In some ways, this 'new brain' is the part that contributes the Reasonable Mind, the logical reasoning element, to our thinking. A major function of the frontal lobes is to make plans in logical sequence and execute them; to judge when one part is finished and move onto the next. During my training as a clinical psychologist, I learned to administer and interpret tests designed to discover whether people suspected of frontal lobe damage still had that ability or not. Being no longer able to plan and switch from one task to another is a grave handicap and certainly adds to frustration and confusion for the individual.

However, that is not the whole story about the frontal lobes. The fact that there is rarely a neat correspondence between one function and one part of the brain has already been noted in Chapter 3 – remember the image of the brain as a rambling bureaucracy? The frontal lobe also governs the function of inhibition and disinhibition mentioned in Chapter 2, and this is significant for anger problems. When an individual who held a lot of anger, but kept it tightly under control through inhibition, sustains damage to the frontal lobes of the brain, they can find the floodgates of that anger opened – not easy for the individual concerned or for those around them.

The frontal lobes also appear to govern our personalities in a way which at present is little understood. Again, brain damage and forms of dementia can lead to seemingly random alterations in personality. A mild and reasonable person can become irritable and impatient, or someone driven and serious can become more childlike and playful. All this adds to the picture of the human 'self' as something fluid rather than fixed. This is an idea that has been put forward throughout this book.

Head injury, brain injury and forms of dementia can indeed add to existing anger problems and produce a problematic degree of anger in someone who has never experienced that before. Also these conditions can significantly hamper the individual in taking control of the problem, as it affects their ability to reach the Reasonable Mind, and so be able to take the long view and not get stuck in tunnel vision. Where disinhibition is also an aspect of the condition, their natural controls are removed. The key here is understanding and support from the people around them, combined with advice from professionals. If family members, partners etc. take into account what the person is struggling with, they will be able to give them space and put up with more irritability than usual. Simple, repeated instructions, combined with patience, help the sufferer to find their way through the fog in their mind.

On the other hand, no one should put up with violence or sustained verbal abuse. In such circumstances, outside professional help is needed. Apart from this, all the stages of dealing with anger that we have covered are relevant in these circumstances, only these are harder for the individual to apply and they will require more help. Where the Reasonable Mind, and therefore the capacity to problem-solve, is badly affected, the most relevant approaches are the physical aspects of anger control, such as exercise and anger discharging techniques, and simple instructions about breathing and leaving the situation to take control of arousal level.

Addiction and substance abuse

As mentioned in Chapter 3, street drugs and alcohol are disinhibitors. Their use makes it much harder to get a grip on anger in a predictable manner. Anyone who has identified that they have an anger problem that seriously needs addressing is well advised to tackle any substance misuse problems at the same time. However, this is sometimes easier said than done. Real addiction takes over people's lives. The substance becomes the priority and everything else takes second place to maintaining the supply. It is certainly possible to escape from this very limiting trap, but it does take effort of will, determination and usually a good reason.

Some of the things that have helped people to escape serious addictions include:

- a vision of how life could be when free of the addiction – one to work on. What are the most important things in your life? Are you really pursuing them now?
- the right sort of supportive relationship. This is not a relationship that covers up for the person and so lets them put off facing the problem, but tough love combined with real, unconditional love.
- anger properly applied can make all the difference. Not the sort of bitter anger that makes you want to escape *into* the addiction, but anger that your potential is being wasted; anger that says you

are worth more than this; anger with the addictive substance that overrides its powerful attraction.

Not all addictions are to substances; gambling, pornography, meaningless sex etc. can play the same destructive role in someone's life and take it over. Even exercise, advocated as a significant answer to chronic stress in Chapter 9, can become an addiction if it is pursued in the wrong spirit. Exercise is attractive because it releases endorphins, meaning it makes you feel good. For some people, this can mean that exercise in pursuit of that good feeling takes over and pushes everything else out of the way. Competition can have that effect also, including competing with yourself. Whatever is important in your life, check that it is not taking over and pushing out the possibility of a calm and well-rounded lifestyle.

The central message is a tough one. Hopefully it is becoming increasingly clear as you progress through this book that managing your anger has a lot to do with facing yourself; facing the ways in which you deal with the world and the ways in which you face yourself. Addiction is essentially about running away from yourself, running away from how it feels to be you now and avoiding dealing with the world. The addiction promises to make everything all right and demands your absolute devotion in return – only the promise is a false one. The addiction usually just adds to the problems. Because of this, and because of the way that addictions disinhibit, the tough message is that addiction needs to be tackled if the addict is to get an anger problem under control.

Mental health issues

We have seen how anger and getting things out of proportion go hand in hand, to the extent that someone sees things completely differently once they have lost their temper. They see things differently from the people around them. They also see things quite differently themselves when they are in a calmer frame of mind. Take a common road rage example. In the heat of the moment, the angry person might see teaching the driver who had cut him/her up a lesson as the highest priority, above physical safety, staying out of trouble with the law etc. Later on, once the Reasonable Mind has returned, they may breathe a sigh of relief that they did not actually manage to corner that driver and confront them.

For some people, that return to consensual reality does not happen so easily. They might feel constantly under threat, and it might be a threat that no one else accepts is real. It is easy to see how, feeling like that, they might confront an innocent bystander whom they imagine is planning them harm. This behaviour and state of mind attracts the label of paranoia. This is taking us into the realm of mental ill health— another area that can have bearing on anger problems.

Along with a growing number of people, I do not see 'having' or 'not having' a mental illness as a particularly helpful or accurate way of classifying what is going on in this and similar situations. As I have written elsewhere, it is more helpful to see mental distress as resulting from people getting tangled up in the process of trying to cope with the challenges of human life (Clarke, 2009). We have already seen in the earlier explanations of how the brain is wired that coping can be difficult. However, where the Emotion Mind takes over in a serious way, people do start to react and behave in ways that do not make sense to those around them; and these ways of behaving and reacting can, in more extreme cases, be dangerous and damaging.

Like the addictions considered earlier in this chapter (*very* like addictions, in fact), ways of coping that are labelled as mental illness can become vicious circles. People can get very locked in and stuck, as that is the nature of vicious circles. Where this leads to anger (and paranoia, for instance, because it is about constantly feeling under threat, can easily lead to misdirected anger), the mental health issue complicates dealing with the anger. Let us look at an example of someone who has received a diagnosis of obsessive–compulsive disorder.

Case study: Freda

Freda was a young woman who had grown up in a somewhat chaotic household. The family was dominated by the problems of her younger brother, who had severe mental health issues, which overwhelmed their parents. Because her surroundings always felt unpredictable and, at times, dangerous, Freda felt constantly under threat. From a young age, she developed elaborate rituals around daily tasks, like washing and dressing. At first these felt reassuring and seemed to make everything more predictable. She felt that if she performed her rituals correctly, nothing disastrous would happen.

The trouble was that the more Freda relied on them, the rituals got more complicated. She found it nearly impossible to get them right and they were taking longer and longer, so getting in the way of ordinary life. When she could not perform them, because her parents were hurrying her, for instance, she feared disaster and became desperate. This desperation came out in the form of anger. Her parents, already at their wits' end with her brother, did their best to allow Freda to do her rituals, but this made her more dependent on them. It was impossible to fit life around them, so conflict was inevitable. As Freda grew from a child into a teenager and then into a largish young woman, her parents became more and more frightened of her rages and sought psychiatric help for her.

It is easy to see that although Freda has a major problem with anger, it would be difficult to address this head-on while she is tangled up with her rituals, and in order to tackle these, she needs the specialist help of the mental health services. Like the person with paranoia, whose fears are permanently out of line with consensual reality, psychiatric medication might well be the first step. In Freda's case, it could be necessary in order for her to find her Wise Mind and to be able to accept that learning to manage without the rituals, though exceedingly difficult, is both possible and necessary. She will certainly need therapeutic help to learn to do this, and at that stage tackling the inevitable anger, as the rituals will not pack up and leave quietly, will be a part of the treatment. So, in exactly the same way as with addiction, an anger problem that is complicated by mental health issues needs to be dealt with alongside the mental health issues.

Maintaining change: mindfulness and everyday life

You might reasonably conclude at this point that you do not have any of the specific problems listed in this chapter: no physical disability, head or brain injury, dementia (yet), addiction or mental illness. If so, good for you, but do take time to reflect on whether there might be something addictive in the way you cope with how you feel inside. Most people have some escape. In its place, this is can be healthy (a walk in the countryside, going for a run, a glass of beer or wine, for instance), but not if it takes over. Be honest with yourself.

Both addiction and mental health issues have in common a breakdown in the balance between the Reasonable Mind and the Emotion Mind. In all cases, the straightforward way to address that problem is mindfulness. Mindfulness enables you to hold the Reasonable Mind and Emotion Mind together in balance. It also happens to be central to taking control of your anger reactions. So this chapter concludes with a look at how you might bring mindfulness into your everyday life in a realistic manner.

While it is important to work at consciously bringing yourself into the moment on a regular basis – hence all the worksheets and reminders – the chances are that there is a lot of mindfulness in your life already without your knowing it:

- an activity that takes your awareness away from the churning thoughts in your head and into the present moment
- anything requiring sustained concentration.

Everyday mindful activities

Here is a list of everyday activities that can be conducted mindfully or are conducive to mindfulness. See what might fit into your life now, or be something to think about introducing:

- following specific instructions, e.g. DIY, sewing or a new cooking recipe
- fishing
- gardening
- a problem or game requiring your full attention
- stroking the cat (or giving time to another non-human).

In fact, this can be whenever your attention is on the activity and not elsewhere. I spend far too much time watching the birds in the garden and the frogs in the pond, but perhaps it is not such a bad thing after all! Such activities are recognized as calming and good for stress relief (provided, in the case of sewing and DIY, it is not too difficult and does not keep going wrong!).

Activities that lend themselves to mindfulness

Routine tasks, such as washing up, cleaning and taking the dog for a walk, are often an excuse for the mind to wander where it will, which means it is likely to end up chewing over irritations (such as having to do the particular activity) and so increase stress. However, with a bit of determination, these activities can be pursued mindfully – meaning that you focus your attention on everything you are doing at this moment in time, and notice in particular everything your senses tell you – what you can see, hear, feel etc.

Mindful activity list

Worksheet 10A

Make two lists:

- one of naturally mindful activities
- one of things you have to do but which could be different if done mindfully

Put a tick beside each item of the two lists when you have tried it, or been aware that you have been mindful when doing it.

Naturally mindful activities	Tick	Activities you could do mindfully	Tick

Use this worksheet to bring more mindfulness into your life.

A thought: one of the attractions of travel is that it takes you into a new environment – everything that you normally take for granted is worth noticing, and the mind wakes up to the present and that feels good. Building mindfulness into your everyday life makes it possible to have that experience without the expense of travelling somewhere else!

So keep working on Worksheet 10A, and notice that 'really living' feeling when the mind wakes up to the present and note that down too when you experience it.

Reviewing behaviour

Worksheet 10B

Carry on with your thought worksheet – the important task of:

- noticing how you think in anger or similar situations
- questioning that thinking, coming up with alternatives.

Date and time	What was happening?	What thoughts went through your mind?	Alternative thought	Belief rating 1–10

Chapter summary

In this chapter you have had the opportunity to think about what has been covered in the book so far. You have also learned how managing anger can be affected by:

- physical injury, deterioration and disability
- head injury, brain injury and forms of dementia
- addiction and substance abuse
- mental health issues.

Finally, we looked at how mindfulness can become a part of everyday life, and you have been encouraged to bring more mindfulness into your life.

PART 4

Practice

Broadening the approach to bring in your relationships and values

CHAPTER 11

Managing relationships differently

Overview

One of the problems that people come up against when working on changing their relationship with anger is other people. The problem with other people is that they are unpredictable. We have already seen that 'ought' is a word much favoured by angry people, and the fact is that other people persist in *not* doing what they 'ought' to. I am not offering any direct solutions to this problem. On the contrary, it is part of the landscape and just has to be dealt with. However, there are ways of relating to other people that help in terms of keeping anger in its place, with the added bonus of increasing your quality of life in general.

In this chapter you will learn about:

- the relationship between anger and assertiveness
- what is and what is not assertiveness
- how to be assertive
- managing the balancing act between keeping a relationship, getting what you want and keeping your self-respect, using the relationship triangle
- the challenge of putting yourself into the other person's shoes.

Monitoring your progress

How is the mindfulness practice going? You will need ready access to your Wise Mind if you are to manage relationships to the best advantage, and regular mindfulness practice is the surest way to achieve that.

Also important are noticing incidents that get to you (even though these might be well below the threshold of actual anger by now), and noticing how you are thinking at such times and coming up with alternatives to any wind-up thinking. This too is an exercise to carry on with until it becomes second nature.

Anger and assertiveness

Some people might question why angry people need advice on assertiveness. Surely, they are only too good at getting their own way! A natural reaction, perhaps, but this point of view is wide of the mark as it misunderstands assertiveness. Angry people get their own way by being threatening and aggressive, and these are styles of communication that are the opposite of assertiveness. Assertiveness means asking for what you want in a calm, straightforward and explicit way. This is not something that can be achieved if the Emotion Mind is in charge, as in angry communication.

It takes a lot more courage to tackle a tricky encounter, where you suspect that the other person will not want to fall in with your agenda, from this Reasonable Mind place. Allowing an angry Emotion Mind to take over appears to lets the angry person off the hook. In a way they are letting go of taking full responsibility for what they are asking for, by being able to claim that the anger just took over.

There is another common situation where out-of-control anger instead of assertiveness becomes the means by which someone gets what they want. The person who keeps bottling out of tackling whatever needs to be tackled finds that their frustration at not getting what they want and need builds up and up. When it has reached boiling point and they lose their temper and demand whatever it is, they are essentially using their anger to enable them to go for it. Only when they are angry enough do they have the courage to ask. To put it bluntly, and cruelly, using anger to mask lack of assertiveness is the coward's way out.

Assertiveness: what it is not

So it seems that true assertiveness is not easy and takes courage. However, there are recognized skills that can be taught to achieve it, and we will look at these now. The idea is that learning to use assertiveness skills will mean that you can ask effectively for what you want without 'using' anger to tackle the situation. These skills will certainly improve your relationships.

The first thing to learn about assertiveness is what it is *not*. There are three styles of unassertive communication.

● **Aggression**

Being aggressive might get you what you want in the short term, but it has serious downsides, and is in fact the opposite of assertiveness.

● **Being passive**

People are often aggressive instead of assertive because it takes courage and skill to use assertiveness. The line of least resistance is to do nothing, keep quiet, let things be. While it might sometimes be a good idea to just accept the situation and make the best of it rather than constantly make a fuss, as a general strategy staying passive means that you will get ignored, side-lined and perhaps walked over. That tends to result in the sort of build-up of resentment that can lead to an aggressive outburst.

● **Being manipulative**

This is the subtle one. Rather than saying outright what you want and running the risk of being told you cannot have it, you try to engineer the situation so that the other person is forced to give in. For example, your (adult) son asks to borrow your car for something specific. You don't want to let him use it as you have reservations about his driving skills, but equally you don't want to tell him that outright. So you book it into the garage for its service on the day he wants to borrow it, and then pretend that you got the dates mixed up when the subject next comes up with your son. As well as being devious, this way of operating will not help next time he asks!

A subcategory of manipulation is indirect aggression. You feel aggrieved but unable to confront the person concerned and complain to them directly, so you get at them in some way which makes you feel vindicated. Plotting revenge (see Chapter 8) comes into this category.

Reviewing behaviour

Worksheet 11A: Unassertive communication styles

Do you recognize these communication styles – in others? In yourself? Be honest.

Jot down some examples. Look in particular for examples of the way you manage situations where you have to ask for something, complain or otherwise confront a difficult situation.

_____

_____

_____

_____

_____

_____

How would you feel about letting go of these ways of communicating?

Assertiveness: what it is

So what is assertiveness? How do you do it?

First, *how* you do it is almost more important than *what* you do. You need to be in a calm, resolute place within yourself. You might care very deeply about the outcome, but you need to ensure that that does not translate into being loud or forceful. Many of the skills covered earlier in the book come in handy here. Mindfulness is obviously the way to bring yourself into this Wise Mind place. Use grounding yourself in your surroundings to keep you there. Notice how you are feeling, what is going on around you and really look at the other person, in an interested and friendly rather than an intimidating way. Breathing long slow out-breaths should reduce excess stress.

What to do:

- Be straightforward and honest – say what you want
- Don't drop hints or attempt to manipulate the other person
- Show understanding of the other person's position while stating yours
- At the start, don't get into argument or discussion – just stick to your point. This is called 'the broken record'; keep repeating your request in a calm and reasonable way, without adding anything or qualifying it at this stage
- Offer something in exchange if possible – people respond to fair exchange
- If it becomes clear that you are not going to get exactly what you want, be prepared to negotiate and compromise if necessary
- Accept the outcome, whatever it is, with dignity.

If you follow this procedure (and it is not easy), then even if you do not get what you want, you can congratulate yourself for having given it your best shot and, equally as important, for having kept your dignity and self-respect. If you are dealing with someone reasonable, the chances are that they will give you what you want next time.

Behaviour changing strategy

Worksheet 11B

Think of a situation or situations that would benefit from being handled with assertiveness. It could be something simple, like returning an unwise purchase to a shop, asking a favour of a friend or making an effective complaint to the neighbours asking them to do something less (e.g. making a racket) or more (e.g. managing their rubbish).

Situation:

_____

_____

Make a plan.

_____

_____

When are you going to tackle it?

_____

_____

What are you going to say?

_____

_____

Is there anything you can offer in return?

_____

_____

If it comes to negotiation, what compromise could be reached?

_____

_____

Managing relationships

The procedure for handling a situation assertively fits well when, for instance, asking the boss for a raise or returning something to a shop, but some situations in which you might want to be assertive are more complicated. You might be fed up with always being lumbered with the washing-up at home, for instance, but aware that your relationship is rather fragile; so if you push the point too vigorously, you might end up having the washing-up done for you on Sunday, but be on your own and without a partner on Monday. On the other hand, is it good for you to be in a relationship where you are always walking on eggshells?

The relationship triangle (Figure 11.1) is a useful tool for disentangling that sort of muddle of priorities. In a situation like that, you need to be clear about what is most important for you: getting

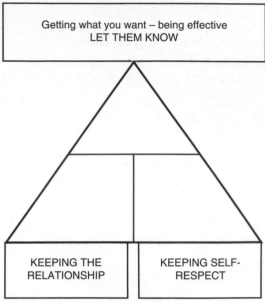

Figure 11.1: The relationship triangle

what you want in the short term, or keeping the relationship? On the other hand, it is always important that you preserve your own self-respect; if the cost of keeping the relationship is having to sacrifice that, is it worth it? These are tricky questions.

The relationship triangle has a section for each of these three priorities. This will help you first to sort out what they are, and then, seeing them set out next to each other, to decide what is most important for you and your life at the present time. Beware of wind-up thinking getting in the way – any thoughts about not letting the other person win, for instance, are likely to be destructive.

Reviewing behaviour

Worksheet 11C: Managing relationships

Consider a current relationship dilemma in your life. Using a copy of Figure 11.1 (see Figure 15.3 for a larger version), work out and write on the diagram what your priorities are.

- Is the main thing to get what you want?
- Is this relationship so important to you that it is worth compromising to keep the relationship?
- You should always look after your relationship with yourself – don't let yourself down and lose self-respect. (In some situations this is more of a priority than in others.)

Which of these three is most important here?

Case study: Bev (2)

We met Bev in Chapter 5. Remember, she was a gay woman who had experienced more than her fair share of rejection and bullying earlier in life as a result of her sexual orientation. She had made the decision to tackle her tendency to go on the attack for no reason as it was becoming a major problem at work. The idea that she could manage her state of arousal and so have a choice about whether or not to act out the anger had appealed to her, and she had had some success in managing frustrations at work more calmly in the short term. More recently, there had been a couple of major outbursts, with no obvious trigger, and her job was on the line again.

As Bev tracked her wind-up thinking, it became clear that these outbursts were not about anything major in themselves, but the result of a build-up of niggles and grievances. The trouble was that she knew no way of bringing up issues that she wanted to address with her employer or fellow employees in a calm manner. She thought she just had to put up with everything. Then, when she lost her temper, it all came out. The trouble was, people then responded by addressing the things that had been bothering her – desks in the office too close together, someone's radio murmuring away the whole time etc. The fact that the tactic worked in the short term made it more likely that she would carry on using it.

When the group reached the assertiveness session, Bev could see clearly that what she needed to do was to apply the skills she had learned to tackle head-on the things that bothered her, straight away, and see if something could be done about it before it became a big issue. She could first attend to her body to pick up early signs of irritation and ask herself what was bothering her. She could then use breathing to get into a calm, reasonable frame of mind, hold her body firmly and confidently, and choose her words to make a request. At the following session she was able to report her first success!

Putting yourself in the other person's shoes

One of the effects of emotions such as anger taking over, is to shut out awareness of where the other person is coming from. The Emotion Mind can shut up the angry person in their own little world where their 'shoulds', 'musts' and 'oughts' rule. Walled off in this rather lonely place, they lose the most important information that anyone needs in order to get on with other people – the ability to work out what it is like for them. Without this, relationships don't work particularly well.

This leads into another vicious circle: the angry person then gets people to do what she/he wants through threats and fear instead of discussing things and working them out together. Because they cannot see the effect that this communication style is having on those around them, they become entrenched in this position, which often leads to losing important relationships. The case study of Gary illustrates this.

Case study: Gary (3)

We met Gary in Chapter 8, coming to terms with helping around the house. He had begun to be more reasonable about that, but he was still a very angry man. He started to notice that he was being side-lined by the family. The children would come home to say they were off to have tea and do their homework at a friend's house. At the weekends, when his wife was home from work and they could have spent time as a family, she took the kids to her parents' house, saying her mother needed help with this, that and the other. Gary started to feel increasingly lonely and irrelevant – and angry; usually he just shouted at them when they were around, but every now and again he went further. He had recently started to pin his wife against the wall to stop her going out yet again; then realized that this was futile and let her go. Another time, he had looked as if he was going for his daughter when she made a particularly sharp, cheeky reply – but drew back just in time.

At the session on putting yourself into the other person's shoes, the group worked in pairs. Gary played his wife while his partner had a go at being an angry Gary. His partner was good at acting Gary, and was realistically threatening when wife/Gary said (s)he was just going to visit her mother with the children. Gary suddenly realized how unpleasant he was to be around; how they were genuinely frightened of him and took every opportunity to be somewhere else, but were too scared to tell him for fear of how he might react.

Gary went home and looked at the family with his eyes open. He saw the fear in the way they looked at him; he saw the way they were around him as if for the first time. He started to make a real effort to be a different husband and father; it wasn't easy, but every time he felt the irritation rising, he reminded himself of the fear in the eyes of the people he loved most.

Gary was helped to see the world through his wife and children's eyes by his group partner's realistic acting, but you can do the same by realizing:

- the other person is just like you; they too have an Emotion Mind
- their Emotion Mind is designed to pick up threat information and get the body ready for action

they mix threat information from the past with what is happening now; you might not be particularly angry at the moment, but if they have had cause for real fear in the past, their Emotion Mind will be expecting the worst outcome.

Applying this to Gary's example, you can see what his wife was going through. She had learned from experience that when Gary got angry he could be at best very unpleasant and, at worst, violent. It was only natural in the circumstances that she arranged things so that she and the children are not around much when Gary was at home. Note that she used unassertive communication, saying that her mother needed her rather than telling Gary why she was really spending time there. Of course, she did this because she was frightened of how he would react if she said it straight out, but the result was that Gary did not get the information he needed about the effect he was having on his family.

That is Gary and his family. Now what about you?

- What does it feel like to be really frightened?
- What is it like to feel under physical threat, possibly from someone bigger and stronger?

We have seen plenty of case studies in this book of someone developing an anger problem in adulthood after having been mistreated as a child. If you know what it feels like to be small and weak and in physical danger from someone big, strong and angry, that could be helpful information in this situation.

OK, now you know what they are going through – what would help you if you were in their shoes? Mindfulness is a really important tool to use to achieve this understanding of someone else's state of mind. But a warning: the following exercise is not easy, especially if you are someone with an anger problem that really affects other people. It takes courage, but it is worth it!

Reviewing behaviour

Worksheet 11D

Mindfully bring yourself into the present moment. Be aware of your physical being, what you can feel and hear. Note what it feels like to breathe, and notice any tension.

Close your eyes and recall a time when you were really angry with someone and expressed the full force of that anger to them. Recall how you felt at the time, and the tension etc. that you experienced. Then let go of that tension and of being caught up with whatever made you angry at that time.

Turn your attention to the other person. What would it have felt like for you if it had been you at the receiving end of that anger? Take into account any differences in size etc. between you. Really try to experience what it was like for them.

If you were in the same situation again, what would you say to them now, and how would you say it?

What did you manage to imagine? What did you learn from that exercise?

Take into account that this is a very hard exercise to do properly. Everything in us that tries to protect us and keep us feeling OK about ourselves will be stopping you from really going there and experiencing that situation. However, this exercise is also one of the most powerful ways to escape from the isolation that anger can create.

Identifying with other people: another way to feel strong

Feeling strong and OK about yourself is important. This feeling might take a bashing when we really face up to the effect we can have on others when we're angry, but putting ourselves into other people's shoes and identifying with them can bring positives as well. This was very evident in the anger management groups. In earlier chapters I have talked about the rivalry that occurred between group members, which often led to some people dropping out when they realized that they were not going to be able to be 'top dog' in the group. As the 12-week course progressed, the group members who were persevering with it started to develop a strong fellow-feeling. They were happy for other members' successes and sympathetic with their struggles. This worked even when members of the group seemed very different from each other at the outset. Do you remember Neville? We met him being advised to seek anger management in Chapter 7. At that point, he was sure that he was right and the rest of the world was wrong. The next instalment of the Neville story illustrates how it was the group that helped him to start to see things from other people's perspectives, even though, with his privileged background, he was different from your average group member.

Case study: Neville (2)

The therapist assessing him for the group had been very uncertain about letting Neville onto the course, but he had switched on his charming, persuasive side and had been accepted. For the first few sessions he appeared to be holding himself aloof, contributing just enough not to be challenged, but simultaneously conveying the message that he wasn't buying it and he was above it all. As the weeks went by, however, things started to change, subtly at first. Neville started to identify with the struggles of the other members of the group against the powerful forces against them, whether it was faceless businesses or heartless partners. This was all the more surprising as there was a considerable class divide between Neville and the rest, and the group represented some of the diversity of gender and race that previously he had shown contempt for. Now he started to see that they were all in the same boat.

As the date of Neville's bullying and harassment hearing got nearer, the others showed concern that he should not lose his job. They could see that his plan to lecture the board on the need to be firm with subordinates and the desirability of robust male humour in the workplace might not help his case. It was the other members of the group who managed to get him to see the other side. One of the women, in particular, explained with passion how she had suffered from a bullying boss and what a toll it had taken on her. As Neville had come to see her as a fellow victim of a heartless world, he was able to hear what she said and to start to approach the hearing in a more contrite and constructive way.

Now it is time for you to apply this approach to your own situation. The next worksheet is more complicated than usual. It is for logging an interpersonal situation – an exchange with another person.

My hope is that you will not have a row with anyone and intimidate them this week, although if this does happen, you can record it here. You might, however, have an uncomfortable moment when you feel annoyed with someone and become aware that you feel like being sharp with them. There is room for that too on this worksheet.

Reviewing behaviour

Worksheet 11E

When it comes to putting yourself into someone else's shoes, there is always a lot of guesswork involved. Nonetheless, think of a recent exchange you have had with another person. Or think of an earlier incident when there was a really difficult situation with another person.

- Think about your first reaction and what you might have felt like doing at the time, even if you managed not to.
- Then guess what would have happened if you had acted in the way you first thought of.

Now consider what you might have done differently, and what the outcome of that might have been.

Date and time	How did you react/ first feel like reacting?	What did the other person experience? And if you had reacted as you first felt?	What might you have done differently? And the outcome?

Chapter summary

In this chapter you have learned:

- about the relationship between anger and assertiveness
- what is and is not assertiveness
- how to be assertive, and how to apply this to situations in your life
- how to use the relationship triangle to achieve a balance between keeping a relationship, getting what you want and keeping your self-respect, and have applied this to your situation
- reflected on the experience of the other person in anger situations and what can be learned from that.

CHAPTER 12

Relating differently to yourself

Overview

In this chapter we are going to look at how you relate to yourself and the impact that this can have on your mood and on your self-esteem. We will apply to it the approach of self-compassion now current in therapy. You will:

● learn to recognize your internal critic, and to treat yourself better
● be introduced to a mindfulness exercise to help you do this
● look for the internal 'false friend' and try substituting the 'honest friend'.

Monitoring your progress

There was a lot to practise in Chapter 11.

First, assertiveness; have you started to notice how you manage situations in which you need to ask for something or to complain? Are there any changes to work on, any successes to report?

Next, the relationship triangle for working out and balancing your priorities. That exercise can be challenging if you come to realize that there is a serious clash, for instance between a key relationship and maintaining your self-respect. Anything learned there? Any situations you were able to think through and manage in a more Wise Mind manner?

And then, how did you get on with the challenge of putting yourself into another person's shoes? If you entered fully into that exercise, do congratulate yourself; it is not always comfortable to face realistically the impact that your anger might be having on other people. That discomfort can have effects on the important relationship between you and yourself, which is what we come to next.

ɔur relationship with you

Ɔo you remember the idea of social hierarchy introduced in Chapter 5? This is the idea that human beings are social primates (i.e. large apes) and that we automatically sort ourselves into a hierarchy, or pecking order. Most of the time we do not notice this because our relationships with the people around us are settled. We have our position in the family (top dog, dogsbody or somewhere in between). We know where we stand at work; it is a good idea to be reasonably deferential to the boss, and one can expect subordinates to toe the line.

In a completely new situation and in some social and other situations, social hierarchy is more fluid. Remember your first day at school? (I do; I was terrified.) Unfortunately, in a school situation, if not well-managed, children can sort themselves into the bullies and the bullied. This social sorting is programmed into our very make-up, and we register it as a feeling long before we get around to working out what is going on. If we are being assigned a lowly position or being excluded, we will feel uncomfortable, afraid or angry. If everyone seems to be looking up to us, it will feel good and help our confidence.

Feeling all right about ourselves and our place in the world is fundamental to a life that is working well for human beings. This has a number of consequences. A major one is that human beings tend to give themselves the benefit of the doubt. This is called the 'self-serving bias' in psychology; see the box below for details.

Self-serving bias

Psychologists have long been aware of people's tendency to give themselves credit when things go well and to blame others when things go badly; this is called the 'self serving bias'. There is much research into the way in which people maintain their self-esteem – feeling OK about themselves – in this way. For instance, a 2004 paper brought together 266 studies from all around the world which consistently demonstrated this effect, although interestingly it is much stronger in western countries than, for instance, Japan (Mezulis et al., 2004).

Some of these studies compare people without problems with people diagnosed with anxiety and depression. Not surprisingly, self-serving bias is lower in people diagnosed with anxiety, and particularly low (though still present) in people with depression. Some research studies have shown that people with depression make more realistic appraisals of their performance in an experimental task (Alloy and Abramson, 1979), leading to the conclusion that it is the rest of us who are out of step! There is controversy about whether a tendency to take the blame on oneself leads to depression, or whether being depressed results in taking the blame and not taking the credit. Whichever is the case, it certainly looks as though having a self-serving bias helps to keep our spirits up – at least in the western world.

This need to feel OK about ourselves is the reason why putting yourself into other people's shoes can be so challenging. People have a sense of what is going to feel uncomfortable, which gives the message 'Don't go there' – all this going on below the level of conscious awareness. That is why you have to be really brave and determined to make the sort of changes covered in this book.

The internal dialogue and putting yourself down

Here the picture gets more complicated. On the one hand there is the tendency to protect ourselves from uncomfortable awareness, which makes it more difficult to recognize where we need to make changes. On the other hand, many people, including a good proportion of those with anger problems, spend their life putting themselves down. Interestingly, it is entirely possible to fail to face up to the real situation while simultaneously putting yourself down. Needless to say, constantly and automatically putting yourself down (as opposed to recognizing the odd occasion when you have got it wrong), is not good. It is another area that requires awareness of what is going on so that you can do something about it. To do this, you need to tune into your 'internal dialogue'.

Internal dialogue is a fancy way of describing when we think as though we were talking to someone else. This gives us a clue to a point that I made in Chapter 1: that all human beings are in a relationship with themselves, and that understanding and working on this relationship is a sure way of making life better and becoming more effective in the world. So, time to notice your internal dialogue!

Reviewing behaviour

Worksheet 12A

What do you say to yourself? Think back over the day.
Have you met any particular challenges?

_____

_____

How did you talk yourself through them?

_____

_____

What are the characteristic phrases that come to mind when you are 'talking' to yourself? Write them down.

_____

_____

Tone is also important. Are you calm and understanding with yourself? Or irritable and impatient? Contemptuous and dismissive?

Your answers should give you a snapshot of the sort of relationship that you have with yourself. If it is one that is less than supportive and understanding, the sections that follow apply to you!

The effect of different sorts of relationship

Now take a step away from your internal dialogue and consider two different types of relationship and the effect they are likely to have on someone.

- First, imagine living with someone very critical who always puts you down. What is that like? What effect does it have on how you feel, on your mood? What effect does it have on your self-confidence? How likely are you to attempt new challenges with that person around?
- Now imagine living with a really good friend; someone who cares about you and wants you to do your best. They are understanding and sympathetic when things are difficult, but they believe in you and so encourage you to take on challenges. What effect does that person have on your mood, on how you feel about yourself and on your self-confidence? How likely are you to attempt new challenges with that person around?

Put like that, it is easy to see that you are not going to be in the best mood or have a chance to really show what you can do in life if you are always around the first sort of person. And if that 'person' happens to be you … well, you are clearly in trouble!

This is not about who is in your household or even who your friends are. It is about becoming aware of how you are treating yourself. The good news is that, as it is about how you treat yourself, you are in the best possible position to change that if necessary.

Many people with anger problems find that their relationship with themselves is more like the first than the second example. This makes sense, and it helps to explain why they spend so much time in a foul mood!

There is a lot of interest in the idea of improving your relationship with yourself in the therapy world at the moment, and 'self-compassion' or compassion focused therapy is an increasingly popular approach.

Compassion focused therapy (CFT)

Compassion focused therapy (CFT) is a fast-growing new approach to add to the bewildering variety of therapies out there (Gilbert, 2005). CFT is important as it goes to the heart of the problem many people have with feeling at ease with themselves. It is another therapy that has been influenced by ancient Buddhist teaching, but also draws on very modern neuroscience. The theory behind the approach looks at brain systems and brain connections. It homes in on the 'affect regulation system', i.e. the parts of the brain that, working together, help people to manage their emotions. As anyone familiar with them knows, small babies are notoriously bad at 'affect regulation'. When something is even the slightest bit wrong, they cry at the top of their little lungs. A comforting adult is needed to supply whatever is lacking, and then to soothe the infant.

If all goes reasonably well, the growing child learns to 'self-soothe' – to manage their uncomfortable feelings for themselves. This does not work well for everybody. Some people are more sensitive than others, and reaching that calm, soothed place is more difficult for them. Also, where a comforting adult was not at hand for the baby, the growing child does not have that model to learn from. Instead, they might pick up harsh judgements from those around them that make it more difficult for them to develop self-soothing. This is a lack that CFT seeks to remedy.

CFT works by engaging people at the Emotion Mind level, using techniques such as imagery to bring a soothing interpersonal situation to life. The idea is that this can activate an underdeveloped self-soothing system within the brain. The 'empty chair' technique is also useful here. This technique relies on the fact that each of us has within ourselves the potential to be several quite different people, depending on mood, context etc. By using the 'empty chair' the therapy client is invited to talk to the part of themselves that needs soothing, as if that part were actually sitting in the empty chair. In this way they can explore how that part of themselves is feeling and learn to relate to themselves in a compassionate way. They then apply this new way of relating in their everyday life.

The approach has been well-researched and outcomes are good (Gilbert and Procter, 2006).

Treating yourself as a good friend

From this it can be seen that treating yourself as a good friend could be an important element in dealing with anger, as it will improve your mood. In addition, it could have good effects on your self-confidence and self-esteem as well. So, how do you set about doing it? I suggest you do it by numbers, recording what you notice on Worksheet 12B below.

1   Notice what is happening now. Start to see your relationship with yourself as if it was a relationship between two separate people. Notice what goes on in the internal dialogue – the way in which those two people relate. In particular, notice any put-downs, times when you have undermined your own confidence in what you can do, which maybe stopped you from attempting something. *Write down the phrases you used.*

2   Having noticed those times, think how you could play it differently another time. Look at the phrases you have noted down from your internal dialogue and ask the killer question: 'Would you say that to a good friend?'

3   It is likely that the answer will be 'No!!' So, what would you say to a good friend in those circumstances? Write it down.

4   Now practise saying this new, friendly phrase to yourself. Do this mindfully. Notice any judgements; we will come back to those. Put the judgements aside. Notice what it feels like to be treated compassionately by you.

5   Next time you are faced with a challenge – maybe something you feel like ducking out of – bring out those 'good friend' phrases. Try them out on yourself. See if you can surprise yourself.

6   Mindfully note the outcome. Maybe you did not manage it after all. Congratulate yourself for trying (remember, you are your good friend). Maybe you did something you had been avoiding, or managed something better than you would have predicted. Congratulate yourself even more. Whatever the outcome, keep working at it!

Behaviour changing strategy

Worksheet 12B

Now follow steps 1–6 outlined above, and record what you notice on this worksheet.

Challenge	What I said to me (critical/ put-down)	Substitute good friend internal dialogue	What was the effect? What did you do?

Judgements and what gets in the way

In the exercise above (Worksheet 12B) I suggested that you note judgements. I know what these are likely to be, because, although there was no self-compassion session in the anger management programme, I have devised and run groups with this focus since then. In the groups the participants have come up with the reasons why they cannot possibly treat themselves as they would a good friend. They would never dream of treating a friend the way they treat themselves, but somehow they are different. Here are some of their objections.

Objection 1: I have always treated myself like that. Can't change now.
Answer 1: Yes, it is difficult because you have had a lot of practice
at the old way. All the more reason to be really understanding with
yourself when trying out a different way that should work better.
Objection 2: It would be selfish.
Answer 2: Not if treating yourself better resulted in you being a nicer,
less angry person to be around – maybe that would be the best present
you could give to the people who matter to you.
Objection 3: I can't treat myself well. I don't like myself. I don't deserve
it. This one is a vicious circle, and so needs a diagram (Figure 12.1) to
explain it.

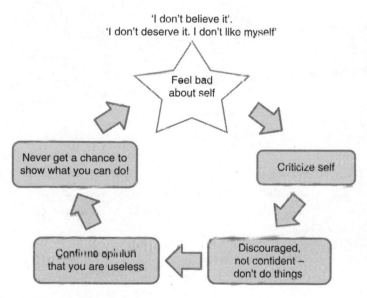

Figure 12.1: A vicious circle

Answer 3: Another diagram (Figure 12.2).

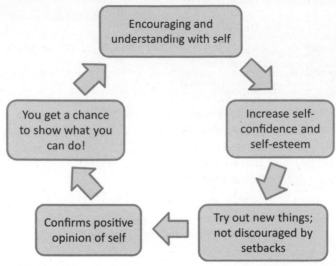

Figure 12.2: A friendly circle

Objection 4: I need to be self-critical in order not to do things I shouldn't do.

Answer 4 This objection has a point. There are circumstances in which you still need to treat yourself in a friendly, compassionate way, but with a bit of added bite. We will look at that in the section on the false friend and the honest friend.

Practical advice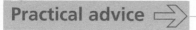

Mindfulness of self-compassion

This exercise is designed to develop your capacity for self-compassion –
to develop your internal good friend.

- Bring yourself into the present.
- Be aware of your body, your surroundings, your breath.
- Note what it feels like to be you, here, now.
- Note your spine holding up your back.
- Note your head at the top of your spine.
- Look around, take your place.
- Feel yourself gathered together, here, now.

(You might or might not wish to close your eyes for the next bit.)

- Be aware of your emotions, how you feel.
- Now turn your attention to how you feel about you.
- Note any emotions that go with that.
- Note where you feel that emotion in your body.
- Note that it is just an event in your body.
- Now get in touch with your loving, caring feelings. (You might need
  to bring to mind someone else, or even a pet animal, in order to get
  hold of these.)
- Note where you feel these compassionate feelings in your body.
- Now turn those caring feelings towards yourself.
- Be aware of how hard you are trying to make changes.
- Be aware of how much support you need in this from the caring per-
  son – who is you.
- Hold that place for a number of minutes, being aware of and letting
  go of judgements and other thoughts.

This mindfulness exercise may be quite challenging and might need
some practice, but it will help you to activate your self-soothing
capacity in order to help you develop your internal good friend.

The false friend and the honest friend

The problem is not always that the internal dialogue is too critical. Sometimes it is too soft but about the wrong things. This might be something potentially addictive: 'Go on, have another double whisky … you've had a hard day'. Or it might be justifying an angry outburst: 'Well, she shouldn't have talked to me like that – she must have realized she had it coming to her'. No doubt the list could go on.

As with the critical inner voice, you can ask the question: 'Would I say that to a good friend – someone I really care about?' In this case it is more difficult. It is much easier just to go along with someone, especially if they are drunk or angry. But if you really have that person's best interests at heart, you might summon up the courage to say, for instance, 'I know it has been tough, but I think you have had enough – come on, let's go home. You will feel better for it tomorrow morning'. Or, in the case of the anger example, 'Don't you think you were a bit out of order there? Perhaps you ought to apologize'.

This response is that of the 'honest friend': the one who believes in you and is looking out for you long term, and so does not want you to let yourself down for the sake of short-term gain. The 'honest friend' sees through the 'false friend' who is suggesting the easy way out. The 'false friend' is, of course, helped along by the self-serving bias mentioned earlier. The 'honest friend' helps you to face up to things.

In the case of the honest friend, the tone of voice, the feeling of the communication, is absolutely key. It is all too easy for this advice to be given in a hostile or contemptuous tone. The message might be the same, but the effect on how you feel about yourself will be very different. Harsh advice given with a put-down will not help you to build your confidence in yourself. If you are to make the sort of changes needed to stop taking the easy option and following the well-worn path, you have to have confidence in yourself and your strength of will.

Reviewing behaviour

Worksheet 12C

Think about your inner voice and about situations where the 'false friend' might be present.

- What does the false friend say? Write it down.
- What would the 'honest friend' say? Write that down.
- Note situations where the comparison might be useful. Try finding your 'honest friend' to help you stand firm, or in other ways make the best decision for you. Note it down.

Challenge	False friend message	Honest friend substitute message	What did you do?

Also, remember to practise and note down your practice of mindfulness of self-compassion.

Mick is an example of how this sort of change in their inner relationship helped someone to feel better about themselves and so be able to manage challenges.

Case study: Mick (3)

We met Mick in early chapters. He had become a bully in self-defence as a boy, because his illiteracy (his problem would now be recognized as dyslexia) made him a target for bullying. However, he was quick enough to learn in the anger management group and worked steadily at making real change in the way he approached life. He was a popular member of the group too. Shy and caring underneath the hard front, other members warmed to him and looked up to him. This in turn had an effect on Mick. He started to see himself in a different light. He was no longer the thick one who had to keep his head down and conceal the shameful secret of his illiteracy.

There was no specific session on self-compassion in that course, but it was clear that it was a change in how Mick related to Mick that had enabled him to come clean in the group about his literacy problem. He no longer put himself down for being stupid. Instead he saw himself as someone with many qualities but with a specific problem that he needed to face and to tackle. So, with considerable courage, he talked about it and the way in which he had until now organized his life to conceal it. Now he was bringing it into the open and had already signed himself up for tuition in order to address it. Because he felt better about himself and no longer simply blamed himself for his problem, he felt able to address it. The group responded with congratulations for his courage in revealing publicly something he had concealed for so long, and felt honoured that he had trusted them enough that they were among the first to know.

Chapter summary

In this chapter we have learned about the internal dialogue and the effect that this can have on your mood, your self-esteem and your self-confidence. You have:

- learned about the self-serving bias and the new compassion focused therapy
- tried noticing how you treat yourself; specifically you have learned to recognize the critical inner voice and the 'false friend'
- tried finding a good friend/honest friend voice to substitute for the self-criticism
- been introduced to a mindfulness exercise to help you to do this
- have learned answers to some of the objections to treating yourself in a friendly way.

I hope this will have put you in a better position to make tough changes.

CHAPTER 13

Your personal rules and values

Overview

In this chapter you will:

- learn about personal rules
- look again at the types of wind-up thinking you slip into most often and use this to uncover your personal rules
- work out where those rules come from
- examine whether they are still relevant, and if not, consider letting them go
- learn about goals and values in order to develop more relevant current rules
- use mindfulness to explore your values
- look at your goals and values, and decide whether they are compatible
- bring all this together to see where you might be going in life.

Monitoring your progress

How did you get on with identifying what your internal dialogue is and its effect, and making it more helpful?

Have you come up with some useful good friend and/or honest friend phrases? The trick is to imagine that friend is in a similar predicament to yourself and work out what you would say to him or her. Then try it out on yourself.

If trying it out on yourself is proving challenging, mindfulness of self-compassion is designed to get you into the mental space where it will work.

If you have managed all that, note carefully any effects that approaching life differently might have had. What is the effect on your mood? On your self-confidence? How you feel now about yourself and other people?

Introducing your personal rules

This is the point where we need to look at what lies behind some of the patterns of feeling, thinking and doing that we have uncovered. A constant theme of the book has been that making change is not easy but it is worthwhile. There are number of reasons why it is not easy. A major reason is the link between anger and personal rules.

These personal rules are the opposite of the sort of rules that are apparent to all. Personal rules usually operate below the level of our awareness, but exert powerful influence from this shadowy position. Wind-up thinking is often underpinned by these rules, making it harder to shift. For instance, those 'shoulds', 'musts' and 'oughts' – where do they come from? Who says it should be that way? Answer: probably you, at a deep level, and then probably someone else before you.

Examples of common personal rules include:

- I must always do it perfectly (or I am a total failure).
- People must show me respect (or …)
- I must have the last word (or …)
- Fairness is essential (or …)
- I must be in control (or …)

The rules get their power from that 'or'. Often it isn't spelt out. It doesn't need to be. It is all the more powerful for an unexpressed threat, lurking in the shadows.

Personal rules tie in with the CBT idea of core beliefs and the linked assumptions or 'rules for living' explained in the box below.

Core beliefs

The idea of personal rules connects with the idea of core beliefs, which is central to CBT. Aaron Beck, one of the founders of CBT, and his associates noted the way that the same thoughts kept cropping up in people's minds when they were depressed or anxious and dragged them down (Beck et al., 1990). They called these 'negative automatic thoughts', or NATs. They asked the question: 'Where do these NATs come from? What keeps generating them?'

They asked their clients to think about their NATs and what these meant for them, and what such thoughts said about a person. In this way they got down to a more fundamental belief that the person held about themselves. Often it was something quite devastating, like 'I am worthless' or 'I am unlovable'. This is the shadowy threat behind the rule. The rule arises because you can't comfortably live with that sort of belief and need to come up with something that will make it all right. CBT calls this an 'assumption' or 'rule for living'. It includes beliefs such as: 'If I always do everything perfectly, I will be valued', or 'If I always manage to please people, they will love me'.

The problem is that these rules are impossible to follow, and by trying to do so you are accepting the horrible core beliefs that lie behind them! It is important to bring all this out into the open and question it.

Bringing personal rules out into the open

For many people, these type of rules have for a long time underpinned their sense of who they are and are how they feel OK about themselves. This is not the sort of thing that it is easy to just ditch, especially if you are someone who tends to feel threatened (common among those with anger problems). However, if these personal rules are maintaining wind-up thinking and so keeping you angry and stressed, they do need to be tackled.

The good news is that bringing them out into the open can often make it easier to see them for what they are – hopelessly unrealistic. Requiring consistent perfection is a recipe for failure, as the world is not like that. Similarly, anyone over the age of about seven should be able to recognize that universal fairness and control are at odds with the way the world works. Hence it is really useful to haul personal rules to the surface of the mind where you can shine a light on them and so see them for what they are.

So, if that is the way to tackle them, how do you uncover them? Again, good news. If you have been logging your wind-up thinking reasonably consistently, you probably already have a fair handle on them.

Reviewing behaviour

Worksheet 13A: Personal rules

Look back at your thought-monitoring worksheets (or start keeping some if you haven't already done so).

Look for patterns. Do your wind-up thoughts fall into one or two of the categories identified in Chapter 7? Remember, they were:

- shoulds, musts and oughts
- all-or-nothing thinking
- overgeneralization (you always …, you never …)
- jumping to conclusions
- you or the world.

You probably found a few were particularly common ways of thinking for you, and these could be the clue to finding out what your particular rules are and where they come from.

First, notice any patterns. Most people have one or two examples of wind-up thinking that occur again and again. Find yours and you have identified your rule(s).

The next step is to work out where they come from. It could be obvious; you might hear a phrase ringing in your ears from a powerful figure in your early life, such as a critical and exacting parent. Or the awareness might be more deeply buried. Hear the phrase in your ear. Is it familiar? Can you hear another voice behind it that might help you to uncover the source of rule? Some people are really surprised when they recognize the extent to which their life has been dominated by a figure from the past.

The chances are that that particular individual, often but not always a parent, no longer features in your life. Even if they do, both you and they have changed and so your relationship has changed. As an adult with your own life, you are no longer dependent on them; indeed, in some cases they might have become dependent on you! Amazingly, such a transformation in current circumstances can have absolutely no effect on the rules and the way they continue to shape someone's reactions, and so their life, long after the person responsible for laying them down has faded into history. This is all down to the Emotion Mind and its trick of keeping the past alive (see Chapter 2).

Then there is the fear lurking behind the rule. What will happen if you don't follow the rule? Often the fear is even less distinct than the rule, but all the more powerful because of this.

However, once you have rumbled what is going on, you can summon your Reasonable Mind and your Emotion Mind together (i.e. Wise Mind) to decide whether and to what extent you want to hang on to the rule and so keep that past alive. This might depend on your feelings about the authority figure who laid down the rule in the first place. In the case of a cruel and arbitrary parent or caregiver, deciding to set the rule aside or sit lightly to it should be relatively easy. Where there was love and admiration in the relationship, perhaps along with fear, it might be a matter of keeping the rule in mind, but not in an absolute way – choosing when and to what it applies, and being prepared to modify it. If the rule is keeping you stressed and angry by feeding wind-up thinking, it would be a good idea to look at it critically regardless of who set it up. Of course, the rule could have been one that you came up with. This is true in Pam's case, in the case study later in this chapter. Here again, a rule that is vital for survival at one period in someone's life can become redundant when the situation changes, but until it is noticed and dealt with the rule remain, causing problems.

Once you have nailed the rule, you can begin to confront the fear. This could be more challenging, but, like the rule, the fear is likely to have more to do with the past than the present, and fear, like a bully, needs to be faced down.

Checklist for tackling personal rules

Look at the wind-up thinking you have identified as characteristic for you:

- What rule or rules lie behind it?
- Where does it/they come from?
- Have circumstances and/or relationships changed over time?
- How relevant and helpful is the rule(s) to your present life?
- Might it/they be dragging you back to the past?

    Take each of your rules one at a time.

- How would you feel about letting go of the rule? Or at least holding a bit more lightly to it?
- What about the fear – does that kick in when you think about letting go of the rule?
- How real is that fear now?
- What would it be like to confront the fear and let it go?

Case study: Jock (2)

Do you remember Jock from Chapter 9. 'I can't let it go because they would win' was the wind-up thought that had kept him stuck. It kept him churning over in his mind that the people who had landed him in jail had ruined his life. The group had helped him to come up with an alternative thought, but it remained a struggle to let go of this sort of thinking. When Jock got to the session on personal rules, he looked back over his thought worksheets. There were a couple of thoughts that tended to occur along with 'Can't let it go'. These seemed to boil down to: 'They are all bastards and out to get you, so get them before they get you'. You can see the fear in there as well -- that they will get you.

This sounded kind of familiar to Jock, and when he cast his mind back his father came vividly into view. Jock tried not to think about his father, a violent and unpredictable man who had terrified the household when he showed up; mercifully he was not around much. The best memories he had of his father were of him teaching him to box, accompanied by the phrase 'You get them before they can get you'. This phrase, along with his experience of home life, had shaped the way that Jock approached the world ever since. The way he came across as a result (hostile and threatening) had of course affected how other people treated him. Jock suddenly saw that despite getting as far away from his home as early as he could, he had carried his father around with him in his head ever since. It was time to notice the old rule creeping into his mind, turning everything sour; time to let it go and move on.

Introducing values

The example of Jock shows the way that personal rules can turn out to be completely out of date, and keeping the past alive in the present. Often this is a past that it would be better to allow to slip away into the past. However, people do need rules to live by, and the best way of ensuring that superannuated ones don't creep back is to work on establishing rules that are sound and relevant in the present. That takes us into the territory of values.

Values are what we live by: what shapes and gives meaning to our lives. Like so many things mentioned in this book, they operate under the surface. Now is the time to bring them out into the open and have a look at them. Mindfulness is a useful tool to help you to get in touch with your values.

Practical advice ⇒

Mindfulness of exploring values

Bring yourself into the present moment.

- Become aware of everything you can sense: what you feel, hear, see etc.
- Be aware of the current concerns filling all the space in your head.
- Gently let them go.
- Get in touch with whatever is most important and meaningful for you.
- Get in touch with your feelings about those people, places, activities, causes and concerns that really touch your heart.
- Get in touch with your hopes and dreams.

Then ask yourself the following questions:

- What things, people etc. are most important in your life. If disaster struck, what would you want to save?
- What gives meaning to your life?
- What hopes and dreams are most dear to you?
- What are the achievements that you are most proud of?
- What do you most want to achieve in the rest of your life?
- How would you like to be remembered? Imagine someone speaking at your funeral about what sort of a person you were and what you achieved. What would you like to be in that speech?
- What do you care about in the wider world? What causes and charities do you support, for instance?

Now come out of the mindful space and write down the answers to these questions. The answers should give you a fairly complete picture of what your values are now.

Self-assessment ✓

Worksheet 13B: Your values

What things, people etc. are most important in your life? If disaster struck, what would you want to save?

_____

_____

_____

_____

What gives meaning to your life?

_____

_____

_____

_____

What hopes and dreams are most dear to you?

_____

_____

_____

_____

What are the achievements that you are most proud of?

_____

_____

_____

_____

What do you most want to achieve in the rest of your life?

_____

_____

_____

_____

How would you like to be remembered? Imagine someone speaking at your funeral about what sort of a person you were and what you achieved. What would you like to be in that speech?

_____

_____

_____

_____

What do you care about in the wider world? What causes and charities do you support, for instance?

_____

_____

_____

_____

Acceptance and commitment therapy and values

Helping people to get in touch with their values has always been an important aspect of therapy, but the approach that has really developed this is acceptance and commitment therapy (ACT) (Hayes et al., 1999). Like dialectical behaviour therapy (see Chapter 2), ACT is influenced by Buddhism and uses mindfulness. (You may be seeing a pattern here, and indeed many of the more recent developments of CBT are based around mindfulness.)

ACT takes the approach that the person who wants to work on change first needs to recognize that the way in which they have been managing so far is getting them nowhere: they are stuck. ACT is keen on metaphors, and uses the image of the person in a hole who insists on digging, or someone in a tug of war with monster, being dragged towards a precipice. In both cases there is a simple solution. For the hole, stop digging and start climbing; for the monster, let go of the rope. In both cases this means having to stop doing the familiar; accept things about the past and present that cannot realistically be changed and make a commitment to set off in a different direction. Deciding what the different direction should be is arrived at by getting in touch with your true values in life and following them. The hole and monster images are often relevant where someone is managing their life and relationships using the threat of their anger. Stopping is hard, because anger works in the short term, but necessary if anything is going to improve.

Broadening your focus

Another way of tapping into your real values is to see that it is a way of broadening your focus, widening your horizons. Being angry can make someone very self-focused. We have seen how looking at a something from the other person's point of view can change perspective. It can take you out of yourself and help you see the bigger picture. The personal rules we identified earlier this chapter tend to have the opposite effect and maintain a narrow focus. Tuning into your values can be like flinging open the curtains and the door to let the light in. The tight walls of the narrow tunnel, focused on resentments and grievances and everything that has gone wrong in the past, dissolves and the things that really matter take centre-stage.

Opening those curtains means a lot of letting go. Remember from Chapter 2 that when your body picks up a sense of threat and switches into fight or flight mode (or 'action mode'), the mind goes into tunnel vision, looking for threat? So the first thing to let go of is that response to a sense of threat. You need to face the feeling of threat and work out what it means from your Wise Mind. From your Wise Mind, you can escape the tunnel vision and let go of the preparation for action – that can take some doing.

You also need to let go of self-focus in order to take in the wider world – that is not easy either. We have seen throughout the book how self-protection, both in the sense of physical safety and in the sense of social position, esteem and respect, are basic to our make-up. It might be necessary to sideline this in the short term. In the longer term, living in accordance with our values usually leads to greater respect from others.

And then our values themselves can pose a challenge, and especially if it looks as though they are at odds with what is going on in our lives at the moment – our goals.

Goals and values

People sometimes get goals and values mixed up. Goals are specific targets that we want to reach. Your goal might be to get a specific qualification, to move to a better position at work, to be able to afford a mortgage, to buy a bigger and more powerful car. Goals are things you can reach. They are concrete and it will be clear when you have reached them.

Values, on the other hand, are never reached. They are usually less tangible things, like fairness, kindness, protection for the weak and animals. Love of family, place and country come into it; ideals like protecting the environment for our children and grandchildren, fighting poverty and disease. Values are less to do with you individually and more to do with how you fit into the overall scheme of things. They are the wider context within which your goals exist. They include religious and spiritual values, which are considered the widest and deepest context of all by some people, while remaining meaningless to others.

However, there is no guarantee that goals and values will fit with each other! A clue to how they might be at odds is given by the Emotion Mind/Reasonable Mind split (see Chapter 2). Goals tend to be something the Reasonable Mind works out. Values belong essentially to the Wise Mind, as they bring in emotion along with reason.

Let's look at examples of when goals and values get in a tangle.

- Example 1 – Think of the person whose goal is promotion at work. To have a hope of achieving that goal they have to work all hours to show how committed they are. Their family, marriage and young children figure prominently in their list of values, yet they hardly ever see their family because they are so busy pursuing the goal; and their partner is getting seriously fed up with the situation.
- Example 2 – Imagine the person whose goal is to buy a powerful car. Maybe when they looked at their values they recognized that protecting the environment was very important to them. Where does that fit with the powerful car?

In both cases, their goals had locked the individuals into tunnel vision so they failed to see the wider picture where their values came in.

On the other hand, you can imagine happier examples where someone's values are about protecting the weak and vulnerable and they enter a caring profession, or about fighting disease and they go in for medical research. Where it starts to get complicated, of course, is where the caring job is too rushed to allow time for proper care, or the research turns out to be more about selling pharmaceuticals. As with so many examples in this book, there is never a simple straightforward answer!

Reviewing behaviour

Worksheet 13C: Goals and values

Time now to apply some of this to yourself.

- First, make a list of your goals, and rank them in order. Rank the goals in importance, making the most important goal 1, and so on.
- Then turn back to the list of values you compiled in Worksheet 13B. Copy them down in the third column. Add any that have occurred to you since, and leave out any that don't really fit the value category (while taking into account that it is not a hard and fast category).

Goals	Rank	Values	Rank

In the next table, write down your goals and values in the order of their respective rankings. Use the final column for:

- a tick if they are compatible
- a cross if they are not compatible
- a question mark if their compatibility is more uncertain, i.e. they are partly compatible, or you are not sure.

Goals in rank order	Values in rank order	Compatibility

Case study: Pam (2)

We met Pam in Chapter 1. She recognized the need to deal with her anger when she felt she could not control her frustration with her new baby. At the same time, she was worried that she would lose parts of her character that she valued, along with losing her effectiveness at her job, if she let go of her anger.

For most of the group sessions, Pam put these questions aside and got on with the challenges of the course with enthusiasm. She relished a challenge and soon she was making significant changes. Her partner, Barry, noted how she was becoming calmer, more reasonable and better able to tolerate the frustrations of being stuck at home with a colicky baby.

When it came to the session on personal rules, Pam started to look deeper. She recognized that her wind-up thinking was all centred around being in control and being taken seriously. She could see exactly where that came from as she looked back to her lonely and loveless childhood, the ignored and squeezed-out child in a family under pressure.

Then she looked at her present situation. She was in a loving partnership, with a much-wanted son who was beginning to grow out of the impossible stage. At work she was valued – they kept in touch with her and were desperate for her return. She realized that the rules that had made perfect sense in her old situation were now out of date. She saw that, with Barry, she was creating something new: a loving family where everyone was valued and there was no desperate need to compete. At work too, she realized, she had earned the respect she was given. There was no need to lose her temper. In fact, she might do her job even better if she stayed cool but firm.

Letting go of the old rules would not mean losing anything – all she had to do was to allow the new life, which was in line with her true values, to grow and flourish.

Bringing it all together: what's driving you?

At this point you should have gathered a lot of information about what makes you tick. This will have a bearing on what makes you angry! Time to bring it all together and discover something about yourself.

Look back at your work on personal rules and where they come from (Worksheet 13A). Where do your personal rules fit with your goals? With your values? What is their role in relation to your anger? Are they the unseen engine keeping the anger alive? This is often the case.

Look at your work ordering your goals and your values and checking their compatibility or incompatibility (Worksheet 13C). Where do your personal rules fit in? Are they closer to your goals or to your values? Or at they at odds with both?

Where do you want to go in your life? Your values should give you the soundest advice here. The ideal position is one where your goals are in line with your values, and your personal rules are not getting in the way.

Does this do away with anger? A resounding 'No!' Chapter 14 will look at where anger might fit into this new and healthier picture. Meanwhile, your homework for this session is to figure out your answers to the questions in this paragraph. That will prepare the ground for making positive use of your anger!

Behaviour changing strategy

Worksheet 13D: Where next?

Where do your personal rules fit with your goals?

_____

_____

_____

Where do your personal rules fit with your values?

_____

_____

_____

What is the role of your personal rules in relation to your anger?

_____

_____

_____

Are your personal rules closer to your goals or to your values? Or are they at odds with both?

_____

_____

_____

Where do you want to go in your life?

_____

_____

_____

Also, don't forget to keep up your mindfulness practice.

Chapter summary

In this chapter you have

- learned about personal rules
- used your wind-up thinking record to uncover your personal rules
- worked out where your personal rules come from and whether you still need them
- learned about goals and values in order to develop more relevant current rules
- used mindfulness to explore your values
- ranked your goals and values in order and explored whether they are compatible
- brought all this together to see where you might be going in life, in preparation for learning in Chapter 14 how to use your anger positively to achieve your potential.

PART 5

Progress

Making your anger work for you

Using anger's energy to fulfil your potential

Overview

This chapter deliberately takes a broader focus. We talked about becoming less self-focused and adopting a broader perspective when discussing values in Chapter 13. This chapter moves the focus away from you and your anger to take in a wider world, in order for you to get the most out of the resource that is your anger.

We will look at:

- anger and the Wise Mind
- the positive potential of wind-up thinking – from 'It's not fair' to campaigning for justice – and non-violent resistance as an example of this
- an example of a positive use of anger in Charles Dickens and 19th-century social conditions
- how to use your anger positively, putting together a plan to do just that.

Monitoring your progress

Where have you got to in reviewing your rules, goals and values? Have you a sense of what is important for you? And of where it would be a good idea for your life to be heading? Have you identified some potential of yours that you need to work on to get the most out of your life?

Once you have got a clear idea of the way ahead, this chapter will offer some indications of how to use your anger to achieve goals that are in line with your values.

Anger and the Wise Mind

Do you remember that in Chapter 1 anger was compared to electricity? Only a few centuries ago electricity was regarded only as a danger (lightning) or a nuisance (static). Since then, we have learned to harness electricity as a current, and it is hard to imagine life without something so useful. Like electricity, anger has potential for harm, and like electricity it also produces energy. It gets the body ready for action. It provides courage to tackle things that it would be hard to contemplate without that injection of adrenaline.

This book has been mainly focused on problems with anger: the problem that the sort of action that anger produces is not necessarily desirable or under your control. Making sure that the action fuelled by anger is the action that you want, the action that will further your goals and values, is the whole purpose of anger management. Anger management is not about doing away with anger, but rather about getting a handle on it and putting it to good use.

However, this aim is complicated by another recurring theme of the book: the difficulty of working out where 'you' are in all this, and even who 'you' are. Deciding what 'you' want might appear to be obvious, but because a human being is such a complex, shifting entity, it is often far from clear. When you are angry and the Emotion Mind is in charge, you might want one thing. Once you have calmed down and the Reasonable Mind has stepped in with its moderating influence, what 'you' want could be quite different.

This is where the balancing act of being human comes in. To be able to use your anger constructively, rather than simply suppressing it (which, as we have seen, can have bad consequences), you need to manage that balance. This means keeping the Emotion Mind around, as you need the energy that the anger mobilizes, but at the same time being fully in touch with the Reasonable Mind. The Reasonable Mind connects with your goals and values, so is able to help you to use anger constructively to achieve the ends that are important for you. If ou recall, the place where the Emotion Mind and Reasonable Mind overlap is the Wise Mind. And mindfulness is the key to accessing the Wise Mind.

Anger and the Wise Mind are a powerful combination. They can achieve great things. Before looking at how you can mobilize this handy source of energy, let us look around at examples of this force for good in the wider world.

Fairness and justice

'It's not fair' has already been identified as a powerful example of a wind-up thought when seized upon by the Emotion Mind. The Reasonable Mind can then tell you that it is not a fair world, a fact you will have started to take on board at a young age. However, the search for fairness, or justice, is not one that should simply be cast aside. It plays an important part in human history and human society.

- What does the word 'justice' mean to you?
- Can you think of examples of injustice that have been put right in the past?
- Are there injustices that you would like to see tackled today?
- What can be done about them?
- Have you ever done anything about injustice, e.g. signed a petition, given to a charity, joined a demonstration?

The correction of injustices can be seen as milestones in human progress. Here are some examples.

- The abolition of slavery, and continuing efforts to stamp it out when it reappears in different guises.
- Giving the vote to everyone, not just rich people and men.
- Equal pay for equal work for men and women.
- The fight against racism, apartheid etc.

These examples and many others unmentioned here have one th.
in common: a weaker group of people who have been suppressed t
those in power gain their rights. There seem to be two universal 'law
here that contradict each other.

- The first is 'might is right'; the strong and powerful will naturally grab all the control and resources for themselves. In playground terms, this is the bully, using his/her anger and the threat of violence to control the weak.
- The second is compassion and fairness; someone who sees this situation of exploitation and feels angry about it – angry enough to *do* something about it.

It is fair to say that in each of these and similar cases of injustice, before a movement gathered force that overturned all the vested interests and the general inertia that kept the unjust state of affairs exactly as it had always been, someone got angry. They got angry about the injustice. They spoke out about it and gathered others to their cause. William Wilberforce and other campaigners achieved this in early 19th-century Britain in the case of slavery; the suffragists and suffragettes achieved it for votes for women in the late 19th and early 20th centuries.

Sometimes the movement for change comes from within the exploited group. They are angry about how they are being treated and do something about it; the trades union movement is an example of this. Sometimes the impetus for change comes from outsiders angry on behalf of the exploited. Where the exploited group is very powerless, as with slaves in the 19th-century America and child-workers, this is necessary. Often it is a coalition of both, as with the anti-apartheid movement from the 1960s to the 1990s.

Of course, the pursuit of just causes does not rule out the use of violence. There is the concept of the just war, though this could be seen as a case of the Emotion Mind (on a national or international scale) overruling the Reasonable Mind. A better example of Wise Mind anger exercised at the level of society is the non-violent resistance movement.

ı-violent resistance

ndhi is recognized as the pivotal figure in the 20th-century non-
iolent resistance movement (Ackerman and Du Vall, 2000). Since
the 17th and 18th centuries, large parts of India had been ruled by the
British, and by the beginning of the 20th century very large numbers of
Indians were strongly opposed to imperial rule. Some of them resorted
to violence. Gandhi, a middle class lawyer in South Africa, took on the
Indian tradition of a holy man and provided leadership and momentum
for a determined, non-violent campaign for Indian independence
(Gandhi, 1961).

Gandhi's campaign included the sort of symbolic mass action that
has become a feature of protest movements. The great march across
India to the sea to make salt, in protest against the hated salt tax, is
perhaps the best-known example. Although it took decades, India was
granted independence in 1947. Gandhi, however, suffered a violent end
at the hands of an assassin in 1948.

Subsequent non-violent protests have drawn on Gandhi's example.
The civil rights movement in the southern states of the USA, under the
leadership of Martin Luther King Jr is a well-known example (Carson,
1981). In the case of the movement to defy segregation on the buses,
Rosa Parks' angry decision not to comply with the unjust restriction
that she could only sit in the non-white section at the back of the bus
sparked a mass protest.

Creativity is frequently employed by protest movements, which
can be linked to the role of creativity as a positive way of discharging
anger mentioned in Chapter 6. The passive resistance of the population
of Prague to the Russian invasion that put an end to the liberalizing
Prague Spring in 1968 made use of flowers and humorous slogans.
Songs and music have been a feature of anti-war protests, and more
recent movements, such as the Occupy protests, have featured masks
and street theatre. Effective communication is an important element in
any protest movement, and a bit of theatre attracts press coverage.

Indian independence and the American civil rights movement are
examples of non-violent action helping to bring about the desired
change. The resistance to invasion following the Prague Spring and,
arguably, Occupy did not. There are no guarantees of success. However,
this is a well-respected tradition that illustrates the possibility of

transforming anger, with its impulse towards violence, into someth
more constructive. Even where it does not succeed, it gets people
thinking – always a good thing.

Before we look at more examples of the positive use of anger, we
shall see how an anger management group member's anger at his son
being treated unfairly was turned to good use.

Case study: Gary (4)

We last met Gary in Chapter 9. He had realized that his family were
avoiding him and excluding him because he was always angry. He
managed to identify the wind-up thinking that was keeping his anger
going and to substitute more helpful ways of thinking.

Now Gary was learning to be part of his family again. He recognized
how much his children needed him, especially his youngest son, Paul, a
shy lad who found it hard to concentrate, was struggling at school. Paul
looked up to his father, but also was afraid of him. Gary made an effort
to spend time with him and got Paul to explain some of the computer
games etc. that he was keen on. Gary was impressed with the computer
skills that he had never realized Paul possessed.

Then the bombshell came. The school felt that Paul was too disruptive
and not making progress, and wanted to transfer him to a special school.
Gary was furious! No one had given *him* a chance at school and now they
were writing off his son – and he felt passionately that this was totally unfair!

His wife stopped him from marching into the school right there and
then, and together they looked at the anger management guidelines. Yes,
there was something wrong with the situation. What was the best way
to deal with it? Gary saw how he might use the passion generated by his
anger to give him the courage to deal assertively with the school – at the
same time as using anger management skills not to simply yell at them.

The couple went to the school together. When the teacher explained
how behind Paul was with reading and writing, Gary promised to help
him regularly with these. Feeling that there was a concerned family
behind the lad, the school promised to give him another chance. At the
group, Gary was able to report that his son was holding his own and
that they were bonding further through the help Gary was giving him
with his schoolwork.

...nkling out the positives
...id the potential

We have seen how 'it is not fair' can be profitably converted into useful assertiveness in Gary's case and, more widely, into movements for justice. Let us look at some of the other characteristic wind-up thoughts.

'Shoulds', 'musts' and 'oughts' are other major culprits, but they too have their uses. They can, of course, point out injustice as well as 'it's not fair'. They also point to a wider sense of how things 'ought' to be, a right order that is often a long way from what actually happens. Along with the injustice of exploitation and inequality, the distress of seeing others suffer can activate those 'shoulds', 'musts' and 'oughts'.

Television brings concerning scenes into the living room, e.g. the misery produced by mass starvation through drought and war, the melting of the polar ice caps with its implications for the future viability of the planet for human beings. Outrage at such situations was the impulse behind the founding of organizations such as Oxfam and Greenpeace, and it continues to fuel support for these and many other concerned charities.

There are plenty of examples of the need for movements like these and response to that need in our own time. However, the detailed example I have chosen of the positive use of anger is from the 19th century; namely the successful novelist, Charles Dickens (Tomalin, 2011). This choice moves us away from the minefield of contemporary politics and, in my view, provides a strikingly clear example. Before explaining how Dickens used his considerable anger as a force for good, we need some context about what conditions in 19th-century Britain.

The social ills of 19th-century Britain

Charles Dickens' life spanned a turbulent period of change for the United Kingdom. The first country to move from a predominantly agricultural economy to a predominantly industrial one, Britain reaped great rewards but also major social problems. The country became wealthy and powerful, acquiring a world-wide empire. The middle and upper classes benefited from this, bringing up large families in considerable comfort with servants galore.

But for the working class it was a different story. The rapid change to an industrial economy drew many people from stable rural communities into chaotic, overcrowded, unhealthy and insanitary cities. There was a reliance on women and child labourers, as they were cheaper to employ, including in the intolerable conditions of the new factories and mines. A population explosion also meant a huge increase in the poor and destitute.

The poor relief system, set up in the 16th century, meant that each parish had helped out poverty-stricken families in their own homes at times when they could not manage. In the 1830s, it was decided instead to build forbidding institutions, called workhouses, where help was only given at the cost of home, family life and liberty, and where conditions were sufficiently dire to deter all but the most desperate and destitute from applying for help.

Most comfortably-off folks managed to ignore the plight of the poor or exploit them, e.g. as cheap servants. There were exceptions, people who were distressed at seeing starving children worked to death and by the inhumanity and studied humiliations of the workhouse.

Charles Dickens and the positive use of anger

Dickens was an enormously successful novelist from the 1830s until his death in 1870. He was able to give a powerful voice to such social concerns, and because of the popularity of his novels, which combined humour and suspense, was able to add momentum to the movements to improve working conditions and regulate the employment of women and children. This voice arose out of a very personal anger which he used cleverly in support of the weak and powerless.

Despite being born into a middle-class family, Dickens knew about child labour from his own experience. When he was 12 years old, his financially irresponsible father was imprisoned for debt, the family was split up, and Charles, as the eldest son, was taken out of school and set to work in a boot polish factory. During this time, he had to live on his own in miserable lodgings.

The young Dickens was angry. He felt keenly the humiliation of being tipped down the social scale. He already had a sense of his own potential, but knew he needed to continue his education to achieve it. He was angry with his parents for not valuing that potential. He was angry with his father, who had a perfectly good income from his job, but spent money as if there was no tomorrow. He had nowhere to put that anger. He simply stored it up – not just as anger about his personal situation, but also as anger for the very many other children in similar or much worse situations, and for all the destitute people he saw daily on his walk through mean London streets from miserable lodgings to miserable work.

Gradually, his circumstances improved, but Dickens never forgot that anger and never forgot all he had learned about the underside of early 19th-century London. He stored it all up, and as soon as he began to gain a voice as a journalist and a novelist, he put it to good use.

In this, he was one of a number of influential 19th-century reformers who together managed to generate a sense of outrage about the worst ills of child labour. They generated enough outrage to get some regulation of it through parliament and to improve living conditions in the cities, for instance, but this took time. The general situation of the poor remained dire, and the workhouses, for instance, survived until the 20th century.

Dickens' tactic was to get the comfortable and complacent Victorian middle classes to identify with the poor not by preaching at them, but by getting them hooked on his melodramatic and action-packed novels. These came out as serials in monthly instalments, with lively illustrations and were the equivalent of today's TV soap operas. Well-written as well as gripping, they are still popular today and are often made into musicals, films and TV adaptations. *Oliver Twist*, *David Copperfield* and *Great Expectations* are among the best known. As well as entertaining, they exposed conditions in workhouses and prisons, the lot of street children and of the poor and destitute in general.

Dickens' intention is possibly clearest in one of his most enduringly popular works, the seasonal short story *A Christmas Carol*. Here, the miserly employer Scrooge is confronted with a series of ghosts or visions that open his eyes to the reality of life for the poor around him, and lead him to provide a generous Christmas for his, until then, desperately exploited employee.

Dickens also took a more direct part in helping those he empathized with so keenly. Wherever he went, he investigated the poorest parts of town, visited prisons and asylums, and encouraged others to do the same. He supported schools for street children and helped families who had fallen on hard times.

In this way, Dickens' anger with his family (who continued to be infuriating) was not taken out on them or turned into bitterness, but broadened out into anger at the plight of the poor and exploited, whose situation he deliberately studied. This anger fired his creativity and was transformed into novels that were both brilliant entertainment and hard-hitting polemic, aimed at righting the injustices at the root of the anger.

Positive anger and you

Charles Dickens might be rather a hard act to follow, but even so it is time now to look at where you might use the valuable energy locked up in your anger to good effect – to make the most of your potential, to follow your dream.

This involves putting together ways of managing anger that we have covered in earlier chapters – a bit like one of those recipes that involve combining different dishes prepared earlier or left over from yesterday's dinner.

First, you need to consider how you might use the new resource of your anger. You might recognize from what has gone before that you are already doing this to some extent – in which case I hope this section will help you to do it even more effectively.

To start, turn back to your work on values in Chapter 13. You were invited to consider the following questions mindfully and then to write down the answers (Worksheet 13B).

- What things, people etc. are most important in your life. If disaster struck, what would you want to save?
- What gives meaning to your life?
- What hopes and dreams are most dear to you?
- What are the achievements that you are most proud of?
- What do you most want to achieve in the rest of your life?
- How would you like to be remembered? Imagine someone speaking at your funeral about what sort of a person you were and what you achieved. What would you like to be in that speech?
- What do you care about in the wider world? What causes and charities do you support, for instance?

You then had a worksheet to fill in, ranking the values in order. You also looked at your goals along with your values (Worksheet 13C).

Now you need to consider what would be a positive focus for the energy your anger generates. Your goals and values should give you clues.

Behaviour changing strategy

Worksheet 14A: Your positive focus for anger

Where might your anger come in handy?

- To enable you to fulfil your potential
- To further some cause you believe in
- To fuel creative expression
- To find your voice

_____

_____

_____

_____

_____

_____

_____

_____

_____

_____

You know now what you want to do, here's some help on how to do it.

- Worksheet 6B, the problem-solving worksheet from Chapter 6, could be useful for creating a practical action plan that will get you from what you think you might do to actually achieving it. Go through the process outlined there and come up with a specific plan, with goals and timescales.
- The section on assertiveness in Chapter 11 could give you a few tips for tackling something challenging, if that is the way your plans are heading.
- The section on discharging anger in Chapter 6 has instructions on how to make use of your anger to take forward your plan. A modified version of the steps outlined there is given below.

p 1a

your anger is live anger, i.e. about something specific, but not
something you can do anything about, notice that you are angry and
use an immediate coping strategy, like breathing, to the point where you
may still be angry but you are able to use that anger in the Wise Mind.

Step 1b

If your anger is ongoing brooding or suppressed anger – the sort that
leads to bitterness – it is particularly good for turning into positive
energy. If you don't, you risk becoming stressed, depressed or just plain
grumpy. Again, notice that you are angry and use a coping strategy that
enables you to use that anger in the Wise Mind.

Step 2

Once you have chosen what you intend to do and are ready to go for it,
you need to drum up the anger a bit by thinking about the cause of the
anger. This is to get your body ready for action, giving you access to all
that energy. This is a balancing act; you don't want to get so wound up
that you lose your temper or go back to the bitter thoughts that just go
around in your head.

Step 3

When you have got started on your positive, value-driven action, let go of
thinking about the specifics of what got you angry. Focus on action and
what can be achieved. Feel good and strong about what you are doing.

Positive expression of anger – creativity

The example of Charles Dickens demonstrates how anger can be
funnelled into creativity, and you don't need to be a Dickens to do that.

Remember how feelings need to be expressed, and none more than
anger. The direct expression of anger is rarely constructive, but you can
use all the tips above to direct its expression.

What means of creative expression comes most naturally to you?

- Do you write? Prose or poetry?
- Do you draw, paint or sculpt?
- Do you make music? Play an instrument?
- Do you write songs? Create DJ sets?
- Do you make more practical things? In wood? Or clay?
- Do you cook? Create recipes?
- Do you design your garden? The decor of your house?

The list is endless. Whatever the medium in which you choose to express that anger, it is guaranteed to add bite and flare to the mix. The right amount will add the extra that gets across to other people. Being able to communicate through your creativity is a bonus. If there is too much obvious anger in there, however, people will switch off. Balance is once again the key. Get it right and you will increase your confidence in your creativity. Try it!

Behaviour changing strategy

Worksheet 14B: Positive anger plan

The purpose of this worksheet is to help you specify your plan, whatever it is, really clearly. You record:

- what value is to be taken forward using your anger
- what problem(s) you expect this to solve – write down your plan of action
- when you will do the activity – be precise
- what outcome you hope for
- what form of creative expression you are going to use
- what means you will use
- what practicalities you have to sort out, e.g. obtaining materials, finding an 'open mike' venue
- what the actual outcome was
- and finally, what happened, with any changes or modifications to try next time. This is about refining your plan based on the outcome.

Value to take forward	
Problem-solving outcome (plan of action)	
When by?	
Outcome you hope for	
Creative expression	
Means to use	
Practicalities to sort out	
Outcome	
Plan refinements	

NB And do remember to keep up your mindfulness practice!

Chapter summary

This chapter has aimed to broaden your perspective on anger and to introduce you to how anger can be used positively. You have learned about:

- anger and the Wise Mind
- the potential positives of wind-up thinking – from 'it's not fair' to campaigning for justice – with non-violent resistance as an example of this
- how Charles Dickens used his own anger to raise awareness and mobilize action about 19th-century social conditions
- how to use your anger positively – whether to achieve your potential, further a cause or for creative expression – and have been encouraged to make a plan of how you can do this.

CHAPTER 15

Keeping up progress

Overview

In this chapter we focus on keeping on with the work and maintaining the changes that you have made. You will learn from motivational interviewing and the change wheel that:

- relapse is normal
- being in two minds is normal.

So keeping up progress will require constant attention, and this chapter provides reminders of the key points from each of the earlier chapters and a worksheet from each to help you.

The change wheel

Getting hold of a self-help book suggests determination to make changes: a resolve to tackle the problem and a seeking for information about how to do it. If you have been following this book as directed, doing the exercises and learning and practising mindfulness, my hope is that you have made significant progress. Now there is no more new content to work through, but you cannot just sit back and put your feet up, I am afraid! Keeping up your progress is hard work, and this chapter looks at how to do that and where to direct that effort.

The process of change and managing to keep it going is summed up really well in Prochashka and DiClemente's change wheel (Prochashka and DiClemente, 1986). They took the view that making change was a continual process rather than a one-off event with a beginning and an end. Choosing a wheel, a circle, as a visual expression of this idea does away with the notion of beginnings and endings.

Prochashka and DiClemente did, however, introduce the concept of stepping onto and off the wheel. The stages on the actual wheel are: Contemplation, Determination, Action, Maintenance, Relapse, and then Contemplation again. The stage of Pre-contemplation is outside the wheel; this is the stage of: 'Problem? What problem?', or in the case of anger, 'Me, angry? I'm not angry', said through gritted teeth and clenched jaw.

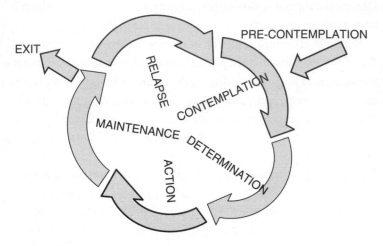

Figure 15.1: Prochaska and DiClemente's six stages of change

The change wheel makes the following important point: before encouraging or helping someone to make changes, it is essential first to work out where they are on (or off) the wheel. If they are in the Pre-contemplation stage, it is futile to give them lots of ideas about how to make changes, however obvious it is to everyone else that this would be an excellent idea. The therapist's task is to make someone uneasy about the present situation, to reduce their complacency and get them worried. Or, in the case of anger, to get them to recognize the problem even if they are still unwilling to take responsibility for it. With r they will become sufficiently worried to pitch themselves onto the wheel at the contemplation stage.

However, at this stage someone is still in two minds and not open to ideas about change. They have to become even more worried so that they become determined to tackle the problem, but at the same time their self-belief needs boosting so that they are convinced they really can make the necessary changes. They can then chug through the Determination and Action stages, arriving at Maintenance -- which I hope is where you are now after reading so far in this book.

But don't get complacent! The next stage of the wheel is Relapse. This does not mean that relapse is inevitable, but it does mean that it is normal. There is a lot of wisdom in the change wheel, and that is part of it. You probably had years of practice of doing things the old way. There were benefits to it, especially in the short term. Change is hard work. You might get tired. Things could go wrong in a really annoying fashion.

If you want to keep on top of your anger and continue to make it work for you so that you can use it to go places, you have to commit to the hard work of keeping up with the work you have been doing. This means keeping this book around and referring to it, remembering the different sections, and using it when things go wrong. That could be when you have a blazing row, or get into a fight or send that sarcastic email that should never have been sent. You need to use these resources to face in your Wise Mind what has just happened and track where it started to go wrong, so that it doesn't happen again.

This chapter is designed to make the work of keeping up your progress easier by reminding you of the important points to remember and keep using. First, we will learn more about the tradition that the change wheel belongs with: motivational interviewing.

...ivational interviewing

...ivational interviewing started as an approach for helping people to ...t free of addictions, beginning with alcohol addiction. It started as a ...reaction against what was the only method for overcoming addiction until then (Miller and Rollnick, 1991). This was the 12-step approach used by Alcoholics Anonymous. The 12-step approach has helped thousands of people to free themselves from addictions to drink, drugs and gambling, and has thereby done a lot of good. However, when Miller started out in addiction treatment, he noticed that there were even more people who did not respond to the uncompromising 12-step approach.

The 12-steps programme requires the individual to admit that they have the disease of alcoholism, to declare themselves powerless before it, and to embrace total abstinence. This offers a lot of certainty, but not much room for doubt and uncertainty. Miller noticed that a lot of people did have the motivation to do something about their drinking, but did not see themselves as helpless alcoholics and so got nothing out of the 12-steps approach. Motivational interviewing was designed to cater for this group.

Motivational interviewing takes 'being in two minds', i.e. ambivalence, as the norm and works with this. The therapist has the task of working with this ambivalence in order to increase motivation for change. Where the client is reluctant to change, instead of blaming them and labelling them as unmotivated, the therapist's task is to increase that motivation.

The therapist starts by allowing the client to expand on the benefits of his/her present state, and listening out for 'change statements' when he/she offers some recognition of the downside. When the therapist sums up the conversation – something all therapists do at regular intervals – the summing-up will start with the benefits of carrying on as before and finish with whatever the client has offered towards change, using their words. For instance, a client with an alcohol problem might expand on the pleasures of drinking and how his/her consumption is the same as everybody else's that he/she knows, but then mention that having blackouts and ending up in a pool of vomit in the gutter is something they could do without. This summing-up is done in the knowledge that people remember best what they themselves said, and also what is said last.

There is a lot more to this subtle approach to manoeuvring people towards change, which has proved its efficacy through research, but there are two points to make here.

- The therapist works out where the client is on the change wheel and concentrates on shifting them to the next stage
- In every communication the therapist should seek to increase the client's self-esteem and self-efficacy.

Only if they believe they can do it will someone embark on the risky adventure of change. You might know something about that.

Keeping up progress and managing relapse

Possibly the most important aim of this book is to help people not to lose their temper, and particularly not to give in to the impulse to use violence or the threat of violence when angry. To stay on track with this basic aim, the chapters you need to keep returning to are Chapters 4–6. Chapter 4, on taking control of your body, is absolutely key. People tend to forget this as they get caught up in the more interesting stuff, like spotting and countering wind-up thinking, later in the course. It is the body getting ready for action without you noticing it that catches you out. Then the Emotion Mind takes over … and who knows what might happen!

another important aim is to help you to learn from your anger. The diagrams in Chapters 5 and 6 are important and worth returning to here. They help you to decide whether your anger is telling you something you need to know about and deal with, and help you to tease out what to do next.

Then there is mindfulness. This is the key skill for getting a handle on the Emotion Mind; being able to attend to it and learn from it without it taking over. In fact, mindfulness is the key to you taking control of your life, and even to you finding out who you are and what you really want.

The later chapters on wind-up thinking and your relationship with yourself and others should play their part in putting anger in its place, while Chapters 13 and 14 give you a chance to understand yourself better and really make your anger work for you.

This chapter provides a guide to what key elements of the book you need to keep up in order to avoid or manage relapse. First, though, a case study of a typical relapse, illustrating the vital importance of never forgetting to keep tabs on what your body is up to!

Case study: Bev (3)

When Bev reviewed her progress at the end of the anger management course, she had done really well. She was managing her anger at work. She had mastered appropriate assertiveness, and was generally getting on better with herself and other people, so that the world no longer felt such a hostile place. She had also just entered a serious committed relationship for the first time as the group drew to its close.

A couple of months later, a request came via her GP: please could Bev see one of the therapists again about her anger. Bev had suffered a concerning relapse. This time, it was not work but, even more worrying, a physical assault on her new partner.

Bev was at a loss about how she could have attacked her partner, whom she really loved. She went through the way in which she had

tried to unpick her thinking at the time and make sense of it. Yes, th...
were details that had irritated her. No, her past history of bullying di...
not appear to be part of the picture this time. Because she could not
understand why it had happened, both she and her partner were afraid
that it might happen again.

It soon became clear to the therapist, as Bev explained her current
situation, that the stress in her life had increased considerably in the
interval. Not only had she taken on a more demanding job, but her
mother, to whom she had never been close, had health problems and
Bev, as the sibling without children, was expected to look after her,
necessitating a long round trip after work each day.

The therapist asked what physical signs of her body getting ready for
action Bev had noticed in the run-up to the attack. Bev realized that
she had not been paying any attention to that aspect. She had tended
to forgot about it as she became fascinated with the later parts of the
course, which seemed more interesting. It soon became clear that this
was a mistake. Because of the stresses of her current life, her body
was constantly near to explosion point. She was prioritizing holding it
together at work and had become good at that. At home, when off her
guard, something minor had tripped the switch.

Bev sighed. It was back to noticing her body, breathing and looking
at lifestyle changes to reduce stress. At least she had an explanation she
could work with.

To help you keep up what you have started in working through this
book, here are a series of worksheets for you to use to keep an eye out
for old habits of thinking and doing and prevent them from creeping
back in.

The introductory paragraph to each worksheet, and the example in
the first row (where there is one), are to give you an idea of when and
how to use each worksheet.

ksheet 15A

tes to: Chapter 2. The past may be getting in the way of the present
ien your reaction to something does not make sense: it is too
xtreme; other people cannot understand why you have taken it so
hard etc.

Date and time	You react in a way that does not make immediate sense	How reasonable is the situation now?	What might it connect to in the past?
	Lisa's partner says he is going to visit a friend on his own. Lisa is furiously jealous and angry.	This is an old friend who is going through a hard time. Her partner has explained this to Lisa.	Lisa's reaction relates to the way she was treated in the past.

Worksheet 15B

Relates to: Chapter 3. Everyone has situations in which they allow themselves to express their anger, and others where they hang onto it (inhibition and disinhibition). When do you let your anger out?

Date and time	Situations in which I allow myself to be angry	Situations in which I don't allow myself to be angry
	Ted allows himself to express his anger at the stupidity of other road users when he is in his car, which means he is constantly at boiling point when driving. So when he's pulled over by the police for a minor infringement, he does not manage to inhibit his anger in time, with bad consequences.	Ted experiences plenty of anger at the stupidity of the other people at work, but he is careful to keep this to himself.

orksheet 15C

elates to: Chapter 4. Are you noticing early enough when your body
s getting ready for action and coming in with immediate coping? The
importance of keeping this up cannot be stressed too much!

Date and time	Physical stress symptoms noted (body getting ready for action)	How I coped
	Feeling tense, rapid breathing, tapping feet or hands, heart rate, getting hot and sweaty, etc.	Breathing Grounding mindfulness Excusing myself and leaving temporarily

Worksheet 15D

Relates to: Chapter 5. Even when you get good at noticing anger starting, it is useful to bear in mind that you have a choice, and noting down that act of decision making can stress the fact that you are in control.

Date and time	Situation and possible choices	What did you choose?	Consequence?

Worksheet 15E

Relates to: Chapter 6. Your anger alerts you to there being something wrong with the situation. Problem-solving is a logical way to work out what you might do about it. Worksheet 6B in Chapter 6 was a good way to do this, so here is a repeat of it. You might want to copy this and keep it around – life will continue to present problems. Once you have stopped acting immediately out of anger, the fact that you are feeling anger becomes a handy way of telling you that a problem has cropped up in good time for you to tackle it.

Brainstorming solutions

Suggested solution	Pros	Cons	Rating

Problem-solving action plan

Solution	Step 1	When by?	Step 2	When by?

Worksheet 15F

Relates to: Chapter 7. The emotion circle is another useful way of breaking down a situation and understanding what is really going on so that you can decide what to do about it. I suggest you draw your own and use them, frequently, whenever something is disturbing or upsetting you, or making you feel angry.

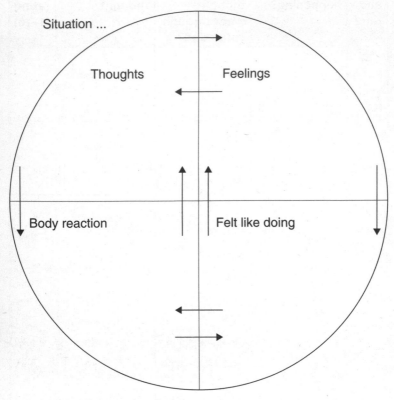

Figure 15.2: The emotion circle

Worksheet 15G

Relates to: Chapter 8. Remember the different sorts of wind-up thinking? Spotting these and coming up with alternatives is something that definitely needs to be worked on. Don't forget to rate the strength of your belief in the alternative thought.

Date and time	What was happening?	What thoughts went through your mind?	Alternative thought	Belief rating (1–10)

Worksheet 15H

Relates to: Chapter 9. This chapter emphasized how important it is to manage the stress in your life. When it builds up, not only is your ability to deal with your anger badly affected, but it also has bad effects on your physical and mental wellbeing.

Source of stress	How to reduce or manage it

Worksheet 15J

Relates to: Chapter 10. This chapter ended with a look at how mindfulness might already be part of your life, and with suggestions to increase the amount of time you spend in a calm, mindful way, by doing ordinary things mindfully: that is, concentrating on what you are doing and really noticing everything about it, rather than just letting your mind wander. This is another way to decrease the stress and increase sound enjoyment in your life.

Naturally mindful activities	Tick	Activities you could do mindfully	Tick

Worksheet 15K

Relates to: Chapter 11. This chapter looked at different aspects of managing relationships: how to be assertive and how to put yourself into the other person's shoes. The relationship triangle is a good tool for thinking about your relationships and how they are working in your life. Perhaps now would be a good time to revisit this and check whether more work is needed in this area, or to recognize that you have got it about right.

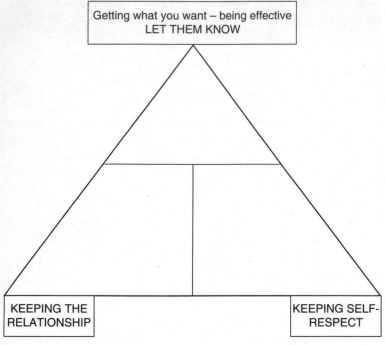

Figure 15.3: The relationship triangle

Worksheet 15L

Relates to: Chapter 12. How are you getting on with treating yourself as you would treat a good friend? Are you noticing the put-downs? The false friend advice? How good are you at bringing in that internal good friend to encourage you and keep you on the right track? Notice times when you need that good friend and notice what you manage to say to yourself. Note those useful phrases below, and note what you managed to do as a result.

Date and time	Good/honest friend advice	What I managed to do with the support of my internal good friend

Worksheet 15M

Relates to: Chapters 13 and 14. These two chapters go naturally together. First, you noted the old rules that have kept you stuck doing things in the old way. Then you considered what is really important in life for you – your values. Finally you looked at how your anger, used in the Wise Mind, can give you the energy and the courage to pursue what is important and meaningful for you in life. This worksheet makes it possible for you to look at these three important aspects of dealing with your anger at the same time.

Old rules I have let go	Values to pursue	Examples of when I have used the energy of anger to follow my values

So that is it! Now it is over to you – to make the most of your life, your relationships and your opportunities. But always keep in mind that you (along with everyone else) are in flux, and there is no boss. There will never be certainty. It is actually more exciting that way. I wish you all the very best!

CHAPTER 16

Useful resources and further help

Overview

This chapter provides links to resources covering the following:

- understanding your body and its responses
- bringing mindfulness into your life
- standard CBT
- newer versions of CBT
- finding a therapist
- further reading.

The body

NHS Choices has an excellent website with a lot of tips and resources about using relaxation and breathing techniques.
www.nhs.uk/conditions/stress-anxiety-depression/pages/ways-relieve-stress.aspx

In addition, I recommend looking locally for resources such as yoga and exercise classes. Sport and using a gym are also recommended.

Mindfulness

NHS Choices has an introduction to mindfulness:
www.nhs.uk/conditions/stress-anxiety-depression/pages/mindfulness.aspx

Mindfulness courses are widely available. If you are interested in it and want to be able to use it therapeutically yourself, the Oxford Cognitive Therapy Centre offers some of the best courses, but there are many others available. www.octc.co.uk

Recommended reading

Jon Kabat-Zinn, *Full Catastrophe Living* (Piatkus, 1996). This book is about introducing mindfulness to large classes of unsuspecting Americans suffering from stress, pain etc. It is a fascinating story as well as being very informative about the origins of the application of mindfulness to emotional issues.

Thich Nhat Hanh, *The Miracle of Mindfulness* (Beacon Press, 1999). This Buddhist monk has written many engaging and readable introductions to mindfulness, but this is one I would recommend.

Standard CBT

The founding fathers of CBT are Aaron Beck and Albert Ellis, and for those who like to go back to the source, the early works are given below. There are many more up-to-date books on CBT at all levels and two recommendations are also given.

Aaron Beck, *Cognitive Therapy and Emotional Disorders* (Penguin, 1976)

Albert Ellis, *Reason and Emotion in Psychotherapy* (Citadel Press, 1962)

D. Greenberger and C.A. Padesky, *Mind over Mood* (Guildford Press, 1995). This CBT self-help manual includes the 'hot cross bun' mentioned in Chapter 7.

Newer versions of CBT

For further information about the newer forms of CBT, I would recommend the following websites. The relevant books are included in the reference list.

Dialectical behaviour therapy (the official website)
http://behavioraltech.org/resources/whatisdbt.cfm
Self-help
www.getselfhelp.co.uk/dbt.htm

Acceptance and Commitment Therapy
https://contextualscience.org/act
Compassion Focused Therapy
www.compassionatemind.co.uk/

Finding a therapist

(Note: this advice only applies to the UK, and is probably most relevant in England.)

Anger management is no longer routinely offered by NHS mental health services. However, some wellness centres and Increasing Access to Psychological Therapies (IAPT) services do offer this. Forensic services and the probation service sometimes do, but I hope you will not be accessing these.

CBT and other approaches for anxiety, depression and similar problems should be available on the NHS through IAPT or an equivalent local talking therapies services. You might need a referral by your GP. In some areas you can refer yourself. If you are accessing an IAPT service, you will probably be offered a telephone interview and possibly phone contact and self-help information initially. If it is considered that you need individual therapy, you will then be referred on for this.

Services for people with more serious mental health problems also usually have therapists available. Most therapy services are overstretched and struggling with higher demand than they can meet, so you might need to be persistent and be prepared to wait.

To access a private therapist, go to the websites of the following bodies and contact one of the therapists on their lists. You can then be sure that you are seeing someone well-qualified who is keeping their knowledge up-to-date and has ongoing supervision. This is important.

For CBT

British Association for Behavioural and Cognitive Psychotherapies (BABCP)

www.babcp.com

For counselling more generally

British Association for Counselling and Psychotherapy (BACP)

www.bacp.co.uk

For applied psychologists

These are often trained in CBT as well as in other modalities, and take a generally broader approach.

The British Psychological Society (BPS), Division of Clinical Psychology (DCP) for a clinical psychologist

www.bps.org.uk

Further reading

There are sources for the topics covered in this book in the References.

My own work is covered extensively on my website, which contains details of my publications, manuals of the groups I have devised and run, and material you can download:

www.isabelclarke.org

This second link contains references to anger publications, anger management and stress management manuals:

www.isabelclarke.org/clinical/anger.shtml

If you have become interested in my more general take on human beings, and in particular (but not only) if you have any interest in religion or spirituality (my main areas), you may enjoy the following book: Isabel Clarke, *Madness, Mystery and the Survival of God* (O'Books, 2008)

If you are interested in reading more about Charles Dickens, I recommend: Claire Tomalin, *Charles Dickens: A Life* (Penguin, 2011)

Worksheets from this book are available free online at www.teachyourself.com/howtodealwith for purchasers of the book.

References

Ackerman, P. and Du Vall, J., *A Force More Powerful: A Century of Non-violent Conflict* (New York: Palgrave, 2000)

Alloy, L.B. and Abramson, L.Y., 'Judgment of contingency in depressed and nondepressed students: Sadder but wiser?', *Journal of Experimental Psychology: General*, 108 (1979), 441–85: doi:10.1037/0096-3445.108.4.441

Beck, A.T., *Cognitive Therapy and Emotional Disorders* (New York: Penguin, 1976)

Beck, A.T., Freeman, A. et al., *Cognitive Therapy of Personality Disorders* (New York: Guilford Press, 1990)

Bradbury, K.E. and Clarke, I., 'Cognitive behavioural therapy for anger management: Effectiveness in adult mental health services', *Behavioural and Cognitive Psychotherapy*, 35 (2006), 201–8

Brewin, C.R., Dalgleish, T. and Joseph, S., 'A dual representation theory of post-traumatic stress disorder', *Psychological Review*, 103 (1996), 670–86

Bushman, B., 'Does venting anger feed or extinguish the flame? Catharsis, rumination, distraction, anger, and aggressive responding', *Personality and Social Psychology Bulletin*, vol. 28 no. 6 (2002), 724–31

Carson, C., *In Struggle. SNCC and the Black Awakening of the 1960s* (Cambridge, MA: Harvard University Press, 1981)

Clarke, I., 'Coping with crisis and overwhelming affect: Employing coping mechanisms in the acute inpatient context' in A.M. Columbus (ed.) 'Coping mechanisms: Strategies and outcomes', *Advances in Psychology Research*, vol. 63. (Huntington, NY: Nova Science Publishers, 2009)

Ellis, A., *Reason and Emotion in Psychotherapy* (New York: Citadel Press, 1962)

Gandhi, M.K., *Non-Violent Resistance (Satyagraha)* (Mineola, NY: Dover, 2001, orig. 1961)

Gilbert, P., *Depression: The Evolution of Powerlessness* (Hove, UK: Lawrence Erlbaum, 1992)

Gilbert, P. (ed.), *Compassion: Conceptualizations, Research and Use in Psychotherapy* (Hove, UK: Routledge, 2005)

Gilbert, P. and Procter, S., 'Compassionate mind training for people with high shame and self-criticism: A pilot study of a group therapy approach', *Clinical Psychology and Psychotherapy*, 13 (2006), 353–79

Gillet, C., Polard, E., Mauduit, N. and Allain, H., 'Acting out and psychoactive substances: Alcohol, drugs, illicit substances', *L'Encephale*, 27(4) (2001), 351–9

Greenberger, D. and Padesky, C.A., *Mind over Mood: Change How You Feel by Changing the Way You Think 2nd ed.* (New York: Guilford Press, 2016), p. 7

Hayes, S., Strosahl, K.D. and Wilson, K.G., *Acceptance and Commitment Therapy* (New York: Guilford Press, 1999)

Kabat-Zinn, J., *Full Catastrophe Living: Using the Wisdom of Your Body and Mind to Face Stress, Pain and Illness* (London: Piatkus, 1996)

Linehan, M., *Cognitive Behavioral Treatment of Borderline Personality Disorder* (New York: Guilford Press, 1993)

Mezulis, A.H., Abramson, L.Y., Hyde, J.S. and Hankin, B.L., 'Is there a universal positivity bias in attributions? A meta-analytic review of individual, developmental and cultural differences in self-serving attributional bias', *Psychological Bulletin*, 130, no. 5 (2004), 711–47

Miller, W.R. and Rollnick, S., *Motivational Interviewing: Preparing People to Change* (New York: Guilford Press, 1991)

Naeem, F., Clarke, I. and Kingdon, D., 'A randomized controlled trial to assess an anger management group program', *The Cognitive Behaviour Therapist*, 2 (2009), 20–31

Problem-solving therapy: www.problemsolvingtherapy.ac.nz/3.html (retrieved 31 August 2015)

Prochaska, J.O. and DiClemente, C.C., 'Toward a comprehensive model of change: Treating addictive behaviours', *Applied Clinical Psychology*, 13 (1986), 3–27

Segal, Z.W., Williams, J.M.G. and Teasdale, J.D., *Mindfulness-based Cognitive Therapy for Depression: A new approach to preventing relapse*, (New York: Guilford Press, 2002)

Teasdale, J.D. and Barnard, P.J., *Affect, Cognition and Change: Remodelling Depressive Thought*, (Hove, UK: Lawrence Erlbaum, 1993)

Tomalin, C., *Charles Dickens: A Life* (London: Viking, 2011)

Williams, M.G., Teasdale, J.D., Segal, Z.V. and Kabat-Zinn, J., *The Mindful Way Through Depression: Freeing Yourself from Chronic Unhappiness* (New York: Guilford Press, 2007)

Index

ACT (acceptance and commitment
    therapy) 102, 191
action mode
    changes 40–50, 116
    dealing with 43–8
action stage, of change 215–17
activities, in everyday life 146–9
addiction 28–30, 142–3, 218–19
    motivational interviewing 218–19
aggression 154
alcohol abuse 9, 28–30, 142–3, 218–19
all-or-nothing thinking 92, 110
alpha males 57
alternative thoughts 109–14
anger
    addictiveness of 19
    grip on life 19–22
    positive use of 200–14
    and Wise Mind 200–2
    and your potential 200–14
anger management
    asking why? 68–70
    group programmes 4–6
    introduction 2
anger trap 12–22
arm/hand muscles, and anger 39,
    41, 117
arousal, and temper/panic 124
assertiveness 127, 153–7

bladder/bowel, and anger 39, 41
blood pressure, and chronic stress 120
body changes, and anger 38–51
brain
    and anger 26–7
    as Reasonable/Emotional Minds 27
brain circuits 14
brain injuries 139–42
brainstorming 76, 226
breathing
    and action mode 103
    and anger 39, 41, 117
    hyperventilation 44
    methods of 46–8

and relaxation 45, 46
and stress 156
broadening focus 191–2

CBT (cognitive behavioural therapy) 4, 10,
    15, 86, 87–8, 102, 104, 112, 136, 184,
    236–9
certainty, and threat 12–15
CFT (compassion focused therapy) 171–2
change wheel, stages 215–17
choices, and consequences 53–9, 225
chronic stress 115–19
    barriers to tackling 125–6
    enjoyable activities 130–1
    and exercise 126–7
    lifestyle changes and 126–34
    management of 230
    and physical health 120–4
    stressors 126–34
    symptoms 224
    worries 126–34
common disinhibitors 28–30
communication problems 140
consequences of anger 53–9
contemplation stage, of change 215–17
core beliefs 184
creativity, and positive anger 204, 212–13

DBT (dialectic behaviour therapy) 14–15,
    17, 63
dementia 139–42
depression 57
determination stage, of change 215–17
diabetes, and chronic stress 121
Dickens, Charles, and positive anger
    206–9
digestive system, and anger 39, 41, 118
disabilities 137–9
discharging anger 69, 76–82
disinhibition 24–35
drug abuse 9–10, 28–30, 142–3

early warning signs 38–50, 53
electricity, and anger 3–4

emotion circle 88–90, 228
Emotion Mind 27, 88, 93, 102, 103, 106,
    116, 123, 125, 144, 146, 153, 160, 172,
    193, 201–2, 203, 220
emotional/sensory memory 17
empty chair technique 172
environment, and anger 28
escape strategies 9–10
evidence, for mindfulness 62–3
exercise 126, 132, 143
expressing anger 79

facial muscles, and anger 39, 41, 117
fairness, and justice 202–5
false friend internal dialogue 178
fight or flight *see* action mode
flexibility in thinking 102–3
focus broadening 191–2
friendly circle, in relationship with
    self 175
frontal lobe brain damage 140–1

Gandhi, Mohandas 204
goals, and values 192–6
group programmes 4–7

head injuries 139–42
headaches, and anger 39, 41
heart, and chronic stress 120
heart rate, and anger 39, 40, 117
honest friend internal dialogue 178
hot cross bun (emotion circle) 88–90
hyperventilation 44

ICS (interacting cognitive subsystems)
    13–14
identifying with others 160–5
immune system, and chronic stress
    120
inhibition 24–35
internal critic 167
internal dialogue, with self 169–80
'it's not fair' response 138, 206

judgements, and mindfulness 60–1
jumping to conclusions 92, 111
justice, sense of 90–1, 202–3

kick-the-cat scenario 25, 31

letting go 103–4, 107–8
life balance plan 133
life satisfaction 132

maintaining progress 215–35
maintenance stage, of change 215–17
manipulative behaviour, as strategy 154
MBCT (mindfulness based cognitive
    therapy) 63
memory
    and time 17–18
    types of 17
mental health issues 143–5
mindfulness 59–65, 130–2, 136, 220, 236
    and ACT 191
    activities in everyday life 146–9, 231
    applications for 63
    and assertiveness 155
    and everyday life 146–9
    evidence base for 62–3
    of exploring values 188–9
    of self-compassion 177
    of thoughts 96
    and wind-up thinking 95–8
    and worries 130
monitoring progress 23–4, 38–40, 52, 67,
    86, 100–1, 115, 135, 152, 167, 182,
    200
motivational interviewing 218–19
MRI (magnetic resonance imaging) 26
muscles, and anger 39, 41, 117
muscular pain, and chronic stress 120
'must' thoughts 91, 109, 160, 206
'my fault' thoughts 92, 111

nervous system 116–19
NICE (National Institute for Health and
    Care Excellence) guidelines 63
non-violent resistance 204
noticing thoughts 98, 101

obsessive-compulsive disorder 144–5
obstacles to progress 137–45
'ought to' thoughts 91, 109, 160, 206
overgeneralization 92, 110

pain, and chronic stress 120
parasympathetic nervous system
116–19
passive behaviour, as strategy 154
perfectionism 127
personal rules 182–97, 234
PET (positron emission tomography) 26
physical injuries 137–9
positive anger 200–14
pre-contemplation stage, of change
215–17
problem-solving, solutions 70–6, 142,
226–7
progress, maintaining 219–35

RCTs (randomized controlled trials) 62
reactions, making sense of 222
Reasonable Mind 27, 106, 123, 142, 146,
153, 193, 201–2, 203
relapse management 217, 219–35
relapse stage, of change 215–17
relationship
and anger 7–9
managing 157–60
with self 7–8, 167–80
types of 170–1
relationship triangle 157–9, 167, 232
relaxation breathing 45, 46
relaxation exercises 44
revenge 104–5
road rage 32–3, 143–4
rules 182–97, 234

self
putting down of 169–70
treating as good friend 173–9, 233
self-respect 107
self-serving bias 168–9
'should' thoughts 91, 103, 109, 160, 206
shoulder muscles, and anger 39,
41, 117
situations, and expressing anger 223
skin problems, and chronic stress 121
social hierarchy 56–7

stages of change 215–17
STEP Past method vii
stomach, and anger 39, 41, 118
stress see chronic stress
stressors see chronic stress
substance abuse 28–30, 142–3
sympathetic nervous system 116–19
see also action mode

temperature, and anger 39
thinking, and anger 39, 42, 118
thoughts
and facts 102–3
finding alternative 101–2, 106
noticing 98, 101
role in anger 86–98, 137
threat, and certainty 12–15
threat system
and the body 16
and the past 17–18
threat vicious circle 43, 160
trauma memory 17
12-step addiction programme 218–19

unhelpful thinking 91–5, 109–11

values 188–96, 234
verbal memory 17
vicious circle
in relationship with self 175
threat 43, 160
violence cultures 30–1
violent behaviour 30–1

wind-up thinking 90–8, 138
alternatives to 100–14, 229
and the past 106
reasons to replace 106–7
and self-respect 107
Wise Mind 136, 155, 167, 193, 200, 201–2,
203, 212, 234
worries see chronic stress

'you or the world' thoughts 92, 111